STOREY'S LIVES

STOREY'S LIVES

Poems 1951–1991

DAVID STOREY

JONATHAN CAPE
LONDON

First published 1992
© David Storey 1992
Jonathan Cape, 20 Vauxhall Bridge Road, London SWIV 2SA

David Storey has asserted his right under the Copyright,
Designs and Patents Act 1988 to be identified as the
author of this work

A CIP catalogue record for this book
is available from the British Library

ISBN 0–224–03308–5

Printed in Great Britain by
Mackays of Chatham PLC, Chatham, Kent

CONTENTS

I

EARLY TIMES

Miners

In the Spring the men made kites:
into the yards behind the houses
they brought shapes
– taller than themselves –
like crucifixes
papered over, the lower surfaces
designed in masks and faces,
effigies
spun out on balls of string wound round axe handles
which shuddered as the kites
sprang up like birds. They rose above the houses
in slow flotillas,
hoisted up in the colliery smoke, floating across the
        estates
and pits and valley to the trees
flanking the hills the other side. Here, like flies,
they stood still. Eyes
turned up in distant farms and copses
must have seen these messages
from the town: fleets of kites
like undelivered letters; masks, faces,
peering down; menaces
which occasionally broke free, waddling downwind to
        the hills and trees,
hanging, a glaring eye, noses,
grinning teeth, amongst the early leaves,
on barbed fences,
or, sodden, sinking in little pools and lakes,
by bridges,
these bloated images

an invasion from invisible men and places,
lives lived in airless spaces
underground.

Blake

At school
a master
describing Blake's tree
seen, full of angels,
when he was five years old
referred to it
as a mental aberration, the evidence,
if such evidence were required,
of an over-imaginative child.

Poor Blake.
Poor us.
Contained by one man's assumption
which made him our master
and us, his boys,
in turn,
the master of poor aberrated Blake.

I see now
years later
who was and was not
the aberrated child.
The master died,
his death a decision
taken long before he tried
to teach us
his particular hallucination
that reality is something
which, communally,
can be registered outside.

And all those boys?
Occasionally I see them
when I go back home
squatting against walls
their haunches
tucked in tight above their heels,
too tired
to look up from
pavements, debt and propaganda:
men who were persuaded long ago
without malice
that trees contain nothing
but their leaves.

Am I now their master?
The epithet has a useless sound,
on the one hand
an alien
on the other
a destitution neither
of us need have found.

Occasionally a glance
reminds us,
the look half-friendly,
half-surprised.
Then the wood comes back:
around us
drifts in
the coldness
of the wary-eyed.

Red and Black

Red and black, my father chats with his neighbour:
just back from work on a morning shift he finds
my mother gasping in the sun, leaning, talking,
pretending fun at his sudden appearance. He laughs

and takes her place. Propped in the back porch,
he reminds me of this morning when I heard him rise,
creak out of their room and move familiarly
through the darkened house. He laughs again,

happy in the sun, squeezing jokes from his tired brain
and reeling off our domestic misbehaviour:
red where he's washed and black where he's missed.
The pit dirt darkens his wrinkled skin. He laughs again.

Grandfather

When he was young he manufactured ropes
in a village on the Yorkshire coast.
They were used for tethering horses, goats,
holding in harvests, fastening doors;
and used to haul in nets
around Iceland, the Dogger, Scapa Flow.

Of thirteen children, eight survived.
Ropes which could tether in a gale
found his family too much a handicap:
now made of metal, spliced by machine,
full of things he had never seen:
oil, hardness, rust.

He sold his shop, packed everything in carts.
He travelled inland, became a miner,
was buried, had arms broken, once a leg,
his back flecked with scars, like marble.
His wife died, his children married.
He moved into rooms and lived alone.

Later, when the bombs began, he sat
beneath our living-room table, looking
up at us with dark brown eyes, his new
white teeth set like fresh saucers
round a smile, refusing to be
moved by bombs and rockets.

Years later, still a child, I remember
being taken down dark back streets,
over lamp-lit cobbles, through eerie alleys,
between puddles and bollards, past
advertisements for coffee, and seeing him
again, in a metal bed, with others like him,

his teeth no longer white – shy, vague:
a look prefaced by war, once, now by age.
Later we received a letter: my father
read it: the same pit, the same disasters.
He looked up: the same dark eyes;
then leant against the door and cried.

Shelter

My father felt the war before it came:
at the end of the garden he dug a hole
deeper than anything we had seen before.
Through grey soil it sank to yellow clay,
darkening finally to a redded orange mould.
Though he dug for weeks he never reached the rock.
Each day when we came home from school
we saw the wedges of clay tossed up,
invisibly projected, swamping the beds
of cabbages and peas, the hole
an enormous monument, inverted.
Each day he brought home stacks of timber
roped to his bike, strips of conveyor,
webbing, nails, taken from the colliery yard
and wheeled six miles through the darkened
        countryside.
They were strewn for weeks about the house and garden
while he shored the hole, dug steps along one side
and laid a roof over the orange cavern,
tarpaulined it, then bedded it down with grass and clay.
Inside he laid a floor of bricks, each
fresh red morsel brought home in a haversack.
He built four bunks,
painted them grey with colliery paint
and made a cradle from an orange box
for a younger brother. Finally he called
us all together and in single file
we trooped down the wooden stairs
into the cell of slowly swinging shadows.
It was lit appropriately by a miner's lamp –
uncanny, as if he'd brought the colliery with him,

a manic actor with his portable stage,
his entombment now a feature of his family's lives:
the smell of tar and wood and clay,
and the yellow incandescence of that lamp.
No doubt he'd had a sanctuary in mind.
It spoke instead of a secret pain,
shadows, the weight of incalculable things outside.

A year later we were woken by the sirens
and sleepily, imagining the slaughter,
stumbled out into the garden, the miner's
lamp lit crazily before us,
my father plunging down the steps
– to cry out, the lamp extinguished,
the place, despite his calculation, full of water.

Lazarus

He came back at night, or in the afternoon, at dawn,
like a soldier from a war.
Entombment, as years passed,
measured out the light he'd lost:
shadows slept where smiles had lived before;
his laugh was qualified with dust.

His life had a steady motion: wheels
wound him down, wheels brought him back;
rocks, breaking other men, broke him apart
– those he had loved, hated: the stones
found no accommodation for his heart:
stone carried to an arsenal of stone,

galleries of rock and coal and shale,
a man afraid to go too deep
that this other depth might keep
him: a distrust made real
in the silence that settled in as, hours
before he left, he began his long departure.

Like a demon in a cage he was lowered down,
his own perennial Lazarus,
and ours, the miracle performed too much
for it to measure either gain or loss:
this buried man, at night, or in the afternoon, at dawn,
faithless, was carried safely back: the coat, the cap,

odd relics of the past,
the smell of coal
and fear: bones, flesh:
the rest he kept
below.
Soon, but for his resurrection,
there was little left to show.

The Pit

I cried for you tonight
and went up to the colliery where you died.
The ropes moaned in the gassy orange flare.
By the lamp room I waited
for you to materialise.

Your shadow might have come:
I followed the lines of the single track,
past trucks and engines;
the shuddering of the rails soon brought it back
– the wooden bridge, crumbled
and bent down in disrepair,
still set for when I first saw you.

It was cold tonight – only yesterday
I'd been thinking Spring had come.

Evening

We sat by the window
talking, I thought, of love.
The light fell on your face:
a frown.
Mine sat in shadow.
A simple division.

You said, 'If you move
to my side the sun
too will fall on
yours.' 'Darkness,'
I said, 'like light, moves
only up or down.'

The sun set.
The light crept
up the pane. 'Blackness',
I said, 'comes
always from below.'
'Warmth rises,'
you said, 'I know.'

Maternal Grandparents

Two heads like polished stones
lie on the pillow,
a single bolster that runs the width
of the brass-ended double bed.

A counterpane unites their bodies,
a faint declivity between
accentuated by the checkered pattern:
flecks of coloured cloth and ribbon,

strands of linen, wool and cotton
sewn adventitiously together
and shaped by a broad black band
around the edge.

A raucous breathing fills the alcove,
on one side of which a door
opens to a yard: a coalhouse
and a lavatory enclosed by a concrete passage.

A curtain normally conceals the bed
from the interior of the room itself,
a frosted panelled door leading on to
and a tiny, two-paned window overlooking

the public path outside. It stands,
the one-roomed home, on a chopped-off
corner: a strange, polygonal
shape, scarcely like a room

at all: perfunctory, a
designer's afterthought, an inconvenient
and unnatural crevice filling in
an otherwise symmetrical plan.

The bed unites them. Caverned
at the eyes and mouth – the cheeks
sucked in and drawing in the air
in which, caught by sunlight,

faint flecks of dust gyrate –
they lie like tiny yellow rocks, embellished,
a medieval tomb of knight and lady,
drawn, a mutual convocation

to this final hour of rest.
They breathe alternately; as
if the bed itself will finally inter,
embrace, create a last enchantment

as on that first night they lay
united by mutual lust and fury,
the inevitable rage of youth and beauty,
their life together framed by children,

hunger, madness, drink and debt:
such unholy lives this couple led
– the light-eyed sanguinity
of the round-cheeked woman,

the languid elegance of that
ancient man – examining each visitor
from across the room, gently,
the eyes expanding, the voice

too quiet, a murmur, raised
in greeting yet indecipherable
– and fading now as, with alternate exclamation,
they pursue each other into death.

The War

He fashioned plans: inventions
first of all for stopping bombers:
a single bomb suspended beneath an English plane,
hanging like bait at the end of a metal chain.
It was hauled into the path of Junkers 88s:
explosions ripped across the page,
spiralling columns of smoke and flame
– swastikas on fractured wings and tails –
while overhead the round insignia
of the RAF embellished on the victor's
side flew on (two fingers
protruding from the pilot's cage).

Like a ball from a bowler's arm,
his next invention was designed
– an oval bullet – to fire round corners:
a trajectory which in his drawings
took matchstick armies by surprise,
men writhing headless, armless, calling,
'MEIN GOTT!' 'ACHTUNG!' 'HIMMEL!' and,
where his German failed him,
'ADOLF: I'M UNDONE!'

A third invention featured two electric wires
dangling beneath an insulated ship:
U-Boats, like shoals of fish,
fled upwards, caught in a morass
of bursting English shells:
'ACHTUNG! MEIN GOTT! HELP ME!
ADOLF: I'M UNDONE!'

Now, grey-haired, he sits alone,
looking up at each arrival,
his face half-reddened by the sun:
ACHTUNG! MEIN GOTT! HELP ME!
ADOLF: I'M UNDONE!

He sits and smiles: departures
find him standing at the door,
weeping, the hand, still waving,
caught, reflected, in panelled doors:
MEIN GOTT! ACHTUNG! HIMMEL! HELP ME!
ADOLF! I'M UNDONE!

Northern Mimes, 1953

i

I would not solicit such infirmities
as those You keep for me,
dear God:
that was his prayer.
What else could you expect
him, among the graves,
to say?
This priest with conjunctivitis
and something funny
with his liver.

It would be nice
to give advice
(like something put on ice
in deference to an ageing lover).

ii

In the street another shadow passes:
the slipping round of the spinning world
greets the slowly rising masses.

The chimneys darken,
the windows sparkle:
used pages from a none
too secret book:
(they drag the curtain
with their glide:
hands manipulate the slide
from plate to plate).

In this street no other features show:
on the clean side
of the pane we watch the shadows grow.

iii

My soul, my soul, how wonderful thou art,
how red, malignant
and apart
from all cheap impediment.

How active, strong and eager to absorb –
how dead and dormant,
reflecting orb,
to all I really want.

My soul, my soul, you know my heart,
you are my censor,
torn apart
from all, my sole preceptor.

iv

He lives the whole time threatened from within:
demons, ghouls, cherubim and seraphim.
In that racked brain the furnaces are lit
beside the Lamb, the Grail, the Crucifix.
Christ carries his own spear now, Judas in his soul:
the fallen and the sanctified lie together on the coal.
The right way is more than flesh and blood can stand,
each man the yes and no of his predicament.

Four-eyes, 1951

An air of fatality – his fate, not ours –
bedecks his brow:
long-legged, thin-hipped, each eye
cast sideways
when the gaze,
otherwise,
might be direct. He moves
with looks averted from his goal,
approaching diagonally those
things which, without his
handicap, we refuse
to see at all.
A strange man who, in perusing us,
is apt to watch the wall.

Advent for a Poem, 1951

Down the street the coaler's cart is brought,
two steaming horses bound within its grasp:
the high, spoked wheels run crosswise on the slag
and scream.
Two white weals are left upon the road.

To feel upset alone brings out the contractor's cart,
word-timbered, wheeled with doubt,
two-shafted monologue of stuttered market pleas
hauled by these wooden forces in equine agonies.

Muscled superfluous to his special task,
four-legged this biped struggles with his load:
realities are shed like shadows in the grass:
bodied like an ape to play
the accompaniment of God.

Haemorrhage

I felt a speck of blood inside my ear
and heard the leak, the holy insect, seep
from this brain carriage into the space
where no bloods creep.

A maggot in the apple of my brain turns round,
consumes the daily refuse of its weight
and slowly from the inside gnaws its way
to the other auricle of light.

Mother

'Oh where has the significance of life got to?'
my mother said.
If it's not where we might expect it
it must be in some other place instead.

Brother

Nothing to give, nothing
with which to part,
consumed and self-consuming
is this cannibal of the heart.

Often he alone survives:
no other sustenance but
the flesh will do: the ripping out
of heart and head.

It comes to this,
it comes to this,
the primal feast,
the communion with the dead,
the hunger of the ghosts
to which his appetite has led.

Prelude

How quickly evil cut off returns
to crucify its victor:
at best the battle is between bad and worse.

No disability quite like this returns
to undermine the house,
hits quite so hard or
is so easy to arouse.

'Vengeance is mine', He said, not for
His sake, I see, but ours.

Pity

Pity is not for sale,
they say, correctly: more
a thing of scale
or privilege negotiated
between the lesser
and the least.

Pity for oneself must
be the first resort:
the look caught
in the mirror,
the tear detected
on the cheek.

Pity for the deceived must
be the next in line:
those who move unwittingly in
channels chasmed out
by those they trust
and think about.

Pity for the pitiless
becomes an even better test:
not for infidelity
itself but for the infidel,
for beauty
not the beast.

All this suggests a soulless face,
pity a barrier
the rich men place
at the door
of the broken,
the faceless and effaced.

Pity's a utensil, then,
the tool got out
with discrimination when
the suffered and the suffering
become a thing
of taste.

Put Upon

These are my friends:
some prefer emnity and hate
— easier for us both —
yet one listens
to their complaint

— to fall for their desires,
numbed by their demands into
having no
corresponding fires.
Soon one is the solitary

credential of virtue, of charity,
even love,
an arbiter as
immobilised as
the one above.

No richness here, no sustenance:
compliance
the only thing, received,
for the ones
who are deceived.

So what? The day comes when they see
someone as distinct as their illness move:
then we'll see
what it amounts to,
this talk of charity and love.

A Philosophy

They are all so certain with their lives:
this one has reconciled himself to God,
this one to himself,
this one has discovered
a synthesis
in which his disabilities
can be viewed
in a more generous and reassuring light;
this one has found
that absurdity
is the proper ground
for his moral rejuvenation;
another has seen how his lovelessness
is a symptom
not of loss
but of his proximity
to a universal pattern.
Another has given himself to looking after maladjusted
        boys.
All have found themselves:
I alone am still in doubt,
the only one left out,
with the years increasingly
afraid;
illumination comes
when everything has failed
– love, self, society, the world:
crushed means for them have clarified the ends.
I can't, without a testament,
I find,
hold on to any friends.

A Man in the House

When I was young,
when I was young,
there were so many things
I should have done.

Here in the darkness monsters groan;
Kings by their servants are overthrown;
Women more in anger than in sorrow
Conceive heroes who die tomorrow;
Today's deaths – sacrifices, too –
Are things that easily one sees through;
While yesterday's deaths are resurrections,
Mistakes made eligible for corrections.
Coldness is a synonym for heat,
And heat is merely coldness less replete.
O, save me from this mad King's charms,
From his lunacy and apoplectic arms,
His kingdom where everything is divided
And nothing for poor sick souls provided.
For my mother, when I was young, once said to me,
'Discriminate: never drown but in the sea:
Rivers, streams and other dilatory courses
Are not contingent with the elemental forces
Which govern you and me (and occasionally your
    father).
Even if the means are insufficient, rather
Than die in pieces subside by preference as a whole:
Disintegration is inimical to the soul
Which seeks the chances
To die in the circumstances
Of a Prince, a Saviour, or a Messiah

(Or something, even, a little higher).
You and me, and several of your aunties,
On my side, though working class, have destinies
Scarcely commensurate with our upbringing:
I hope in you we are instilling
A sense of secret dignities and rights
– Not like your father's side, the lights
Of which I hope we'll never see again,
Who have wet blotting-paper for a brain.
Please, please, my son,
Don't fail me like your father done.'

       O, O, O,
       when I was young,
       when I was young,
       there were so many things
       I should have done.

Morality

I have an aunt who married for money,
an uncle who did the same:
it took them a fortnight to discover their loss,
a lifetime to lay the blame.

You might have thought they'd have taken more care
to examine each other's estate,
but where wealth is concerned not happiness
there are few who hesitate.

In the end, my aunt and uncle
had to look for manna above:
failing to find it here below
— they were condemned to a life of love.

Away Match

They came out in twos and threes,
not running,
nor walking,
each muscle casually displaced,
one index
– a leg, a hand – as replaceable
as another.

The sky darkened, running
in crevices
overhead: thunder.
The ball rose above the silhouette
of cooling towers and chimney: a head
gazed up,
one arm couched, crooked.
Figures fell.

The light moved:
limbs fashioned from the morass
of mud and rain: a solution
of earth and blood: one
standing in isolation
staring at his feet.

In the mirror by the door a head
leans back,
turns, regards
the world outside:
a bird rising from a rock.
The shadows flicker
on the panes. A face dissolves:
three more miles.
A hand folds up a pack of cards.

He moves slowly to the tune:
girls gather at the bar.
Across the hall someone
breaks a glass.
At home his wife sleeps by the fire.
Someone laughs. He lights a cigarette.
Outside it's begun to rain.
'My dance.' If only
it could be played again: astonishing
how fame brings responsibility.

Sportsman

A misshapen giant at
the age of thirty-two
still running with a
ball as he might
a quarter of that
age in a not
dissimilar costume
along a beach,
marking his descent
into a life which,
lived too early,
he did nothing
to prevent.

Family Life

Sis came down and said,
'No more she'll go a-roving, then,'
and Ken said,
'Mother's gone?' and
cried into his hand
and said,
'In a better place than this.
Poor Mam.'

Mr Macauley came and took her
measurement which he had taken
once before
and came back hours later
with a box which he put our
Mam inside. And then,
Poor Mam, she'd had a happy
life, he said, no cause for
grieving there.
And then,
'My men will take care
of all arrangements,
Steve,' referring to my father by
his christian name since years before
at school they'd been close friends.

Only dad had gone into
the pit and Mr Macauley into
coffins which he sometimes supplemented by
making beds for outsize gentlemen and ladies
– one at least, our Ken had said –
and chairs and tables
which he sold in an annexe of his shop.

'She was a fine old lady,
Steve,' he said,
and went back home
to fetch a wreath which my
dad had ordered for Mrs McGaherne
who had died the day before
and whom we knew as a fine old lady
too only
for the past few years she'd lived alone.

'Ah, well,' my father
said, 'perhaps they'll meet. You never
know,' and then, 'What lies
beyond the grave is anybody's guess,'
and then, 'Poor Mam, she was a mother
to you all
and to me the finest wife that ever
lived. Ah well.'

He sat beside the driver
on the day
who had known my father
as a boy
and who, as we were leaving for
the church, had said,
'Remember Charlie Constantine
who fell off a lorry and split his head?
He's a county councillor
now.' 'Not Constantine
with bright red hair?'
'Sure, that's the man,' the driver said.
'Temper, too, to match,' my father said. 'You'd
never guess these things before.
Used to pittle by our
hedge and showed off parts of his anatomy
to passers-by
which could have landed him in trouble quite easily,'
my father said.
'Damn lucky fellow, Constantine,' they said.

And then between the gates
and up between the plots.
The clay stuck to the heels of Sis's shoes
and Ken said, 'They should have had a board at least.
God damn and blast this bloody place,'
and fell with his hand into such a mess
that his suit was never clean again. 'Ashes
to ashes,' the man in the cassock said,
while father cried.
The hole he had for tears
was never stopped until we reached the public house
and in the Private Room he sang, 'O, may we meet
on that further shore.' Sis got
married after that
and Ken went into a home
and I in turn was taken off to Pennyfeather Hall
for boys whose parents were either
dead or
unable to look after them at all.

Dad lived alone
until one
night he fell in Sis's room
which he'd used since our poor
Mammy's death with no one
to help him or
to cook his meals at all.
'He missed your poor
old Mam,' a neighbour said,
coming out one day
to say
that poor old Dad was dead.

The Hall

This is Breakdown Hall
and these are Breakdown People:
the ones you see inside
are recalcitrant and feeble.

He is the one you trust
to love you if you must:
the rest are only able
to talk to you at table:

they sit and knit and read
and holler when you bleed:
bellow for the doctor,
for the beadle and the proctor.

O, take me back again
to where I've always lain,
in silence and alone,
like a piece of precious stone,

reflecting, unreflected,
rejecting, unrejected.

This is Breakdown Hall
and these are Breakdown People:
the ones that seem so small
are the ones who've not been able

to measure out their lust
in the quantities they must.
Standing by the stair
are the ones beyond repair.

(Standing in the doorway
are the ones who never surely
will ever see their lives in
one whole piece again.)

O, take me back again
to where I've always lain,
in silence and alone,
like a piece of precious stone,

reflecting, unreflected,
rejecting, unrejected.

This is Breakdown Hall
and these are Breakdown People,
the ones who only see
the altar and the steeple:

they are the ones who know
how despair and anguish grow
like flowers in the night,
blossoms out of sight:

the ones on whom the door
is closing more and more,
until that final shout
shuts all their loved ones out.

O, *take me back again*
to where I've always lain,
in silence and alone,
like a piece of precious stone,

reflecting, unreflected,
rejecting, unrejected.

Gone Mad

Sit round the symmetrical, square-shaped room:
      a plastic palm on a plastic table
set (with dying leaf) in the middle of the floor.

Each one of us is mad:
      not 'mad' as the axeman or the drunk is mad
but as a climber slipping his last hold
      might fall:
the cry that greets us when we rise
      or sleep.

Each one of us at intervals is called:
      'What dosage are you on?'
      'How is your mood?'
What's to do?
      We pick and choose
epithets, images:
      'Like falling off a cliff.'
'Like being shot.'
      'Like being drowned.'
'Like being murdered.'
      'Like going mad.'
'What is mad?'
      The doctor smiles.
'If we knew that with certainty.'
      He smiles again,
benevolent,
      winsome,
empathetically removed.

Despite his uncertainty I know it well:
      it turns you on your head,
      it pins you to the bed,
no more communicable
      than a dream,
confusing in its form
      – 'I floated from a tower' –
but not in its effect:
life moves in incalculable ways,
      contracts,
expands,
      leaves relics of its passage:
the animated matter that each one of us presents
      in guise of our distress,
crying on the edge of endlessness.

Mother, Mother

Just before it all began
she took a knife and
would have stuck it in

through her,
through me:

how rarely two lives
with one stroke
could disagree.

Walking back from work he couldn't have known
what the wifely
greeting was to be:

a kiss,
embrace:

his beloved waiting in the porch
to demonstrate her prowess
with a blade:

her life
and mine.

What held her back?
Two lives contained
in a single sack:

an embryo;

some six months cargo,
the ship as well.
How could she refrain?

mother,
mother,

a single flame, light
flashing from a windowpane:
nothing else is seen. O,

mother,
mother,

why didn't you try
and save us both
such misery?

A deftness more alive than dead,
the paradox she always fed
by the give-take of that blow withheld

from her,
from me.

Bred in a tomb,
in a tomb conceived,
that knife the only liberation
either would receive. O,

mother,
mother,

what held you back

from you,
from me?

How rarely two lives
with one stroke
could disagree.

Our Lady's Prayer

Our Mother,
         who art in hell,
Blasphemed be thy name:
Thy purgatory be sustained,
Thy intention be exalted
In this world and the next.
Deprive us this day of sustenance,
Retrieve in us our evil
As we retrieve the evil in others;
Return us to temptation,
For thine is the damnation,
The pain and the terror,
For ever and ever.
                    Amen.

Thoughts from Highgate
Cemetery, 1957

i

A city, he'd said,
that was last invaded
nine hundred
years ago:
the only one, so
far, attacked
by rockets: Freud and Marx lived
here, Shakespeare, Darwin, Newton,
Milton:
here revolutionaries lived
in peace . . .

it seems incredible at first that Christ
endured his passion in another place:
no doubt the Immaculately Conceived
took this into consideration:
better deceived
by the ill-at-heart
than welcomed
by the well-intentioned.

ii

A place as near to death as anyone can find:
they all come here who would have it known they'd
        died,
those wishing to be sanctified
by public acclamation:

subvertionists and vipers, psychopaths and whores:
among so many cheats and rogues
those who go in for killing-vogues
are provided with protection.

iii

His head is larger than the rest:
the others, at best,
sport only angels, clothes
folded, in one instance,
on the grave,
hands raised to save
and sanctify
these less plebeian souls.

iv

What will be left? A line of bone
and of the brain
little else but dust and stone,
the frame
of one thought leading to another.
And of all those games he played
– a father, son and lover –
nothing: except the spot where one limb has stayed
the dust, held back a space
and in the earth a gesture
maybe measures out the trace
of flesh, of blood: a creature
still to those who can
recognise in this the emblem of a man.

Afterwards

Soon the miracle begins:
the odd look, smile, that
precedes the last
embrace and touch;
the way the hand falls
to retrieve her clothes,
the mouth half-pouting
as she restores
each breast
to its tiny canopy;
her jumper – her head rising
from its folds,
querulous at
being watched, enquiring;
the feet slipped in
the shoes; the last
look up to see what
conclusions have been drawn.
None:
except that here the miracle
begins; the incredible
and fantastic
put back
in place. Maybe
it's a drink, or
a cigarette,
but when she goes out
through that door
who could tell that
she's been loved and that
I, lying
here, am still loving?

Samson

Last night his hair was cut
and this morning, passing the shop,
he saw the bins being carried out:
across the top

of one was strewn a wad
of hair, the debris of a hundred skulls,
like some eclectic genius gone mad
– grey, brown, black, curls,

strands: a demonic head
carried high across the street
and flung into a cart, crushed,
and driven off. Where do one's debris start?

Where do one's pieces wander?
Hair, nails, faeces, breath:
a cart, a furnace, river, sewer:
carried off, in death,

ending the same
as we began: sand,
sea, components, indistinguishable from the rest, of
        flame
and air and land.

Domestic

The cat is an animal everyone adores
save those enveloped by its claws:
twin instruments, its teeth, like vices,
to crush, betwixt them, little mices.

Vast clams, its eyes, to close and open
on scenes from which its enemies are hoping
to be excluded: yet little hope exists
for those who surely must resist
the menu they most plainly offer
betwixt cat's waking and its supper.

O cat, o cat, do not despair,
for I alone shall be your fare
as out of tins your food I give
to distance death that you might live.

Graffitist

On this bareness he inscribes
his inexpressible asides
as, channelled from a deeper source,
they neither mend nor stop his course
to perdition – nor, more, prevent
what, until now, no circumvent-
ing power had presence to distract:
the unspoken evidence he had cracked:
(sprung open at the seams, beyond repair,
to be moved by grief to his despair)
– until such words as these pronounced
what by no other means could be announced:
living, as revealed to him,
both source and punishment of sin.

Lupset, 1967

Now, when I go back, there is no one
there at all:
in the field children
playing with a ball;

caught at a window
suddenly a look
— set at a distance then and, now,
thrust further back,

a last excision.
And on that gate
a fresh name, scribbled more in
haste than hurries on the fate

about to overwhelm it; habit
a thing that muffles every door:
man and wife and child live in it:
histories pour

out from every nook and crack:
nothing that these past
faces in old houses see, the back
of one man shadowed by the last.

Little of the mould remains:
bare walls and tiles,
a broken latch, the scuff and stains
by every door and sill, the piles

of slack strewn out across the yard: old people save
the slightest thing that went before:
birth, racked nights: the wave
of a departing hand outside the door.

Piano

Upright, it stood against the wall of our living-room,
unused, its maker's name arranged in a golden arc on
the centre panel. No one
had the skill to play it:
in a house of miners and professional athletes passivity,
like sitting, was considered something of a woman's art.

It appeared quite early in my parents' lives:
a present. As one child
followed another, it collected dust,
photographs, toys and magazines:
here my father ate his meals,
standing, stubbing out his cigarette.

One day he trapped his fingers in the lid:
like a misdemeaning animal
he dragged it to the door,
crashed it down the steps and,
as if this revenge had a long time been
intended, attacked it with a hammer.

It lay on its side to receive the blows:
a mad percussion sprang through its gaps and holes
– a chisel and a saw, followed by an axe –
a tune of such velocity and violence
that people collected in the road: no one had heard
before a rhapsody played with such peculiar venom.

It took him a week to complete his composition,
his audience waiting as he strode each evening
from the porch. A fire, finally, burnt out its heart
— its members bursting, torn apart.
At the end of the week my father stood alone
amidst blackened ash and screws and wires.

Years later, eroded by fatigue and fear,
he came home from work to find his son, muscled for
the tasks that drove him to his knees,
painting by the fire: a picture of clouds,
a girl, a line of trees;
found, too, drawings kept secretly in books.

That famous look again:
trapped fingers in the lid:
hammer (chisel, axe and pyre),
dismemberment, blackened bolts and
screws, dark effigies of wire:
the ashes sing, and nothing dims the fire.

Wakefield: November 1972

A lake covered this land below the castle
in neolithic times; artefacts
have, over the last
few years, been prised out
of the sandy soil: bone hooks,
stone daggers, arrow-heads:
a smoothly-rounded stone through
which a single hole
has been roughly pierced.

Where hawthorn and weeping willow
grew beside decaying vegetation
in the marshy pools, terraces
have been moulded to
the underlying contour of moat
and keep, the wild, denuded
debris, dog-toothed, fanged
by wind and rain, protruding
from layers of uniformly mounded grass.

A single tree stoops over the pool
where refuse mouldered
amid reeds and crumbled stone
and mud. Pathways that wound
between shrubs, through clayey canyons,
dipping to the inner moat
before the steep ascent to the flag-staffed
keep, have gone. Nothing remains
but a smooth enclosure of cultivated grass

and these protruding stone embrasures
like remnants of the rock itself:
an empty window gazes to the west
where, caught in the fading
light, the leaded furrow
of the Calder flows across
the dale where those neolithic
hunters came, crouching
to the water's edge.

More recent swords and spear heads
and the chippings from a suit of mail
have been dug out from the field below:
cannon-balls, horseshoes; while,
still shadowed in the grass, lie
the sand-bagged enclosures
of the anti-aircraft guns which,
three decades ago, caught
aircraft circling to the south.

A dog crosses the slope, disappears
beneath a hedge, then re-emerges
in the field beyond, the flattened
debris, unploughed, from a harvest
three months gone. The past
takes on new meanings as the years
recede: here boys played games
and never thought of those pale faces
gazing out to where the river melted

in the sun's last rays, the forest
darkening beneath the Pennine ridge;
nor glimpsed robed figures
mounting broken stairs, crying
in cold rooms, nor
predators crouching by a lake
whose contour is marked
by an ashy track on
the flatness of the fields below.

A tractor tugs out the earth
beside the river: between the nearest houses
and the bank itself mounds
of dark brown soil, ribbed by tyres,
rise in pyramids above a central pit
where lorries from the town
tip streams of paper, ash and cans:
dust, mingling with the smoke from scattered fires,
drifts to the smoothness of the castle hill.

A highway crosses the valley to the west.
Lorries and cars glide down
its shadowed slope: too loosely
imprinted, the vanished lake,
too far away, the castle
mound, to be other
than a faint enigma that,
like this distant figure, flaws
the grandeur of these wooded hills.

A Town Not Unlike His Own

In his youth the bare-foot children
padded dirtily along the street
to where,
fair-
roofed,
the recent brick-built
houses stood:
a constellation that,
in crescent, avenue and road,
lit the hill-clad sky at night.

(Writes material in his –
how would he describe it?
– dispellation,
enquiring, why
        (unshoeless, craftily-attired
– jacket, skirt or suit, jeaned)
should they,
        in these re-resurrected streets,
recall
        a vision
he had known before?)

Stood and waited,
sat and thought
(sought)
that he alone were still alive:
animal that he hated –
mother to his bride,
father to his expectation:
self to his other
(rein and reason gone) –
Apocrypha:
suffix to his prefix,
prefix to his pride.

Neville

i

I don't know why I ran from home
(the place we run to all our lives),
                              whenever, as a child,
I reached the door;
                              dare-tortured by the thrall
of leaving, not of coming in
                              ('turning to nature'
as I ventured to the Park,
                              'to nurture'
as I stole from shops).

I don't know why I ran away,
                              and have been running all my life
— running to the edge of things
                              where need
seems more than need itself is worth,
                              as if,
in disassembling truth from recklessness,
                              I am running to my birth.

ii
I'm not sure how well
    I know him:
a vacuity,
    once occupied
by dream and doubt
    — by knowing
he was not,
    then was —
not what he was
    but what his absence
meant,
    inspired,
drove on to:
    a vacuity
that the mind must populate
    with thoughts of you
as imaged by
    my thoughts in you,
or you in me:
    the celerity
of reason that conducts sense
    from senselessness:
to reach my mind
    in thought of you,
imaging the imageless.

iii
A glimpse I catch
of what
was there: not
so much
a shade, a glow:
a passing
light, glaring,
gone
amongst the grieving
all this time.

Autumn Songs

i

This autumn day I have
named the dead.

Brother, o be true:
let me,
in my life, live through you;
let me
your singing now attend:

o sing your song,
o sing your song of living, love: not

'This is wrong' but
'This is true'
to all that you
have suffered through.

ii

Neville is this strange disturbance
I once knew:
at my conception
took his leave: Brother,
let me sing through you!

Redresser
of my wrongs and rights:
the well-fought-for,
the well-run-to,
the figuration that made clear
that mourning never
dies but here:

let's have it out,
your great rejoice,
your final shout:

o let me hear,
o let me hear!

iii
I am very much aware
of where
I stand because of you:
my darkness is your
light. I hear your
singing in my voice:
'O now rejoice,
o now rejoice!'

This is the life-song
that I knew,
your singing in
the night, your
singing when that singing clear
brings me to sing your singing here:
'O now rejoice,
o now rejoice!'

                              iv
Rests in that love
and would not sing
until I brought
my love to him.

Rests on that shore
until I spoke
and to him
all my friendship took.

Rests in that mind
that I might tell
his heaven found
despite my hell.

Rests in his home
that I might sing
all that I cherish
and adore in him.

Rests he in me
and I in him
that we might share
our suffering.

Rest we at ease
that we might please
the friendship and the love
we seized.

Rests he at peace
that I might waive
the life I lost
for him to save.

O Neville be my friend.

Child

The child in me is
younger than I thought:
younger as the foetus curls
to brother dying:
the misadventure.

Nothing older than
this creature
curls to mother
sighing, dying
into verse.

II

A SCENT OF RAIN

Bells

The bells, the Sunday bells ring
not from our church which is in decay
but from the Cypriot Greek establishment
which has taken one of 'ours' and
transformed it into 'a testament of faith':
the only one to make a sound
as musak figures out from
pub and bars: 'Taken in by Christ'
has more
to it than meets the eye in
a place where noise equates
with passion, peace with hell.

Can't tell
what the sound of bells proclaims:
gullibility, naivety, 'the primitive mind' where
'primitivism', like Christ, can be taken
either way − a state of mind
confirming that the 'soul' is 'here',
not 'there', is 'now', not 'then'.

What faith to measure bells by
now on our merchandising day of rest
where bells are rung by those
                              who play least part
in our occidental world
                    of tart and tout:
the electronic hiss and thump
compressing into mind and heart
as if for wrecker to provoke
that final cry:
'O come, dear God, and be my friend'?

Without Extremes

Without extremes,
       we feel those things
that civility intends:
       extremes diminish ends
to right and wrong —
       this grieving for effect, or
half a truth, or
       a half-realisable truth
which, without extremes,
       appears a truth itself:
as if contentment is the home
       we otherwise would never know,
nor dream about,
       nor shape,
nor share,
       havering to extinction,
talking to our death.

Dying, Else

Little so he knew
        save how
                he felt:
cornered. Spoke
as he saw, saw as he heard:
conjunction of the two
                made
                    sense.
Chose 'out of line' when,
                  finally,
he knew
        what mattered less,
or even mattered not at all:
the line of living as he felt,
of dying 'as you fall'.

Things

Reflection and dissemblement,
          jaded yet pronounced,
sharp-shuttered to the share of things,
raised reckless to the 'way things are'.

What 'things' are they
          that have their say
no matter what we do or don't,
that kill and cull,
          depleting and enhancing some
in one swift burst of will or won't,
          cancelling health and beauty out
in drain and drag of pain and pout,
          the inoffensive round
when things end in a shout
          – a cry of how they were
or might have been:
          the pallor of the caring flesh
fleshly no longer as it's carried out?

Wind

A breeze blows sheets
      of paper on the bed:
sets
      three aside, leaves
one exposed – 'What is
      the point' – the writing's
in your hand –
      'of resolving a mystery which,
of its nature, eludes
      resolution at the same
time as it provides
      the means by which
such a mystery might
      be resolved?'
You have it right:
      a surmise of why we,
at the end,
      know less:
pinioned
      on a nail as
Christ to suffer loss,
      not us
to reassure but,
      betrayal as
he suffered then,
      his boss.

Breeze

I like it in the evening
when the breeze comes in, stirring
paper, here, where I work, turning
a page, drifting
one across the floor, as if reading
(about itself, as much as not), as though writing,
with that stirring
in attendance — the sky darkening
in the yard outside: the air, disturbing
and disturbed, cajoles, measuring
the movement that its move unfolds, distilling,
however far it comes, whatever it may, in touching,
bare, all it bears in upon, distressing,
arresting
dread, conveying
the coming
of what was bound to come, conveying
death or that first breath as touching
on a woman's breast its invisible caressing.

Guilt

The sky is clear:
    no stars,
nor moon:
    windows,
       curtains drawn,
blank against the brick.
Traffic on a distant road
       echoes where the mind is still
busy,
    musing in the dark
on warmth and custom,
       where still,
if near,
  far off
    are hopes
passionate
   for
    forbearance.

No Longer There

What do you want:
                fatigue as well as animation,
eyes cool as ice yet warmly framed,
                mouth grimacing to pleasure,
the irascible drive of passion,
                pain:
the formation of each gesture
                displaced
by expectation,
                by formulation,
condolence, sympathy,
                the rest,
the trajectory of feeling
                spent,
then dying
                − dying in a shout, a cry,
a pledge
                − until the present or the past
runs out −
                framing on a kiss,
a sigh −
                invisibly,
unmoved,
                'no longer there'?

87

Scent of Rain

The scent of rain comes to the window:
      the night is still:
the trees stir in a sudden breeze,
      falter invisibly, stir again,
then still:
      nothing moves.
Moments ago I left you in our bed,
      came here,
subdued:
      the arbitrariness of what we feel
leaves us forgetful:
      what do we measure
but the pace at which we part,
      our only gauge
of where we are,
      of what we do — of how
fatuity and boredom play their part,
      absolve themselves
and guy
      our living merely that we may not die?

Love

I wonder how beautiful she looks when I'm not there:
Do others see her beauty when I'm gone?
Are they as transformed as I am by her spell?
Her look, her glance, her words
                dictate what I should do.
I move in the space that she allows.
                She grants me wishes:
I may see her.
                I may not.

Does she love me when I'm gone?
Like I love her when she's not here?
Do I love her as she is,
                or as she was when I was there?
All I love is what I feel.
What I feel I feel from her.
She gives me love to give it back:
Lends me her beauty for return.
Endlessly, I hand it on.
At no moment does it stop.
Loving, I discover, never ends.
I love love loving her. I love.
Love loves, loves she I love.
I love.
                Is she still there?

Need

First there is the need and then the source
        by which that need is gratified
by giving of resource
        to have that need revivified
— as opening of that need to need in turn,
        each need appeased by need's return.

So I love you that you love me
        to the end of all eternity
— unless I find in someone else
        a need more needful than yourself.
Wherein in need a greater source I find
        much greater than the one I leave behind.

So love succeeds as in the sum
        of need needing need, ad infinitum.

Inspiration

In the mornings she wrote:
                at midday she left, on foot,
to see her lover.
                From his roof,
                      scattered with geranium and
                        poppy,
                    fig and fuchsia,
she could see the town,
                the district where she lived,
in a declivity,
                beside the river.
Here, in the midday heat, they sometimes lay,
                shielded by a hammock,
swifts and swallows overhead,
                voices from a distant road:
the stillness as they talked,
                made love.

At the sound of the homeward city
                from the street below
they went downstairs and watched the news —
                conflagration,
                    child-abuse,
                    a politician misconstrued —
each in wraps, his head across her thigh,
                her thigh beneath his hand.
They watched:
                much of what they learned they loved:
what it was to be alive —
                armaments,
                    the collective whole,

                        barbarism,
        much control:
                        the individual counted.

When she left they kissed,
                        made their next appointment and –
shadow on the roof and in the street –
                        she walked,
                                for exercise,
back to the district where she lived:
                        signs of riot,
                                a burnt-out shop.
Rested from the afternoon, she wrote –
                        marks,
                                stains,
like the geranium and poppies,
                        the fig and fuchsia,
                                shades and furies,
                                red, vermilion,
flurries of her love
                        petalling each page
                                like the imprint of a dove.

On the Roof

Geranium and poppy:
        we lie,
regarding the variegated colours,
        red, puce,
vermilion,
        as if the love
this tall roof
        brings
serries out
        in plant and flare
of petal
        as one slow colour
measures light
        fleshly
on each stem
        and sways as,
in movement to another pulse,
        we lower and,
lingering on each flourish,
        swear
that nothing that we feel
        can, in these petals, share
this chalice of delight.

All Moves

In the night
       a crack of wood,
unplaceable,
       across the room,
reminds that movement is
       the flow of thing to thing,
sharing,
       shaping,
wearing us,
       taking us
to what we come from,
       what we are.

Everything moves,
       everything in motion,
the lintel, arch and frame
       in motion:
moving in the part that dies,
       decay
matched to decay: we move
       — move with the motion
called out of parent into light,
       that first slow move of love.

Flowers

All the flowers on your roof
are, as we know it, proof
that how and why and where and when
act as addenda to our stratagem
of love that touches love and grows
as plant to plant imprudent shows
more than all but loving sows.

How came it, why is it, where is it, when?
are realities that pale to irreality, then:
no more than shadows, as space and time,
lost in the weave and weft of rhyme
that transfigures not only but subsumes
the sense that sense, in sensing you, assumes.
We love, therefore, as flowers in season,
as love that loves, my dear, with reason.

Night

You move: in motion as a siren
wails across the backs. Water
from a neighbour's fountain
brings in the scent of rain,
cooling as the breeze that springs,
sudden, in the night, and stirs.
Sleepless, I turn, admire your brow,
the motion of each breast. How
still you are: moments ago
you spoke as — roused — hours before,
we wakened to disturbance in the street.
The curtain caverns with the breeze:
sails in the room, then out, the muslin drape
of light dissolving into shade
as if in movement to your breath.
How much I love you, unaware,
when dreamed-of and dreamer
coalesce to keep in one
the dream that I, in dreaming, dream upon.

Sentiment

Sentiment alone keeps us
afloat: have you considered this,
how thinking-not leaves us
the space to come upon the spell
of living in one vowel
turned in live to love;
and how this magic serves
in living love
or loving life so well?

Cool Air

In the cool air an accordion plays:
a voice calls: hands clap. The tune, broken,
is suddenly resumed, moving in the room
as the day moves in the shade,
brought in with the smell of cooking,
laughter — brought in with the breeze,
drawing the day down to a cooler end
— drawing as our fingers, earlier,
lightened, drew,
to make our movement one.

Sleep

You move, stir
in your sleep:
your lashes flicker where,
on your cheek,

the tear dries:
an insignia from when, awake,
you signalled what was
wrong, now right, your phrase,

'Our loving has gone wrong',
now right as the breeze goes right,
into us, reviving
motion, the beat

and bluster that covets
you in sleep, the preparatory force,
breathing, this breeze,
from another source.

Pillow Fight

There's savagery in the way we love:
something of rapine — the cry,
the penetration, the clasp,
as if we jointly reach, one
in the other, to disassemble
what is tender, subtle, true.

This is the game and more
we play in simulation of what
we show when, calmly, we undress,
display: something of the rapist
not in me but you: this figuration
that sees the serpent enter
at your thigh and exchange
its look inside your eye.

Addenda: dissatisfaction in the way
we separate what shall be yours
from ours; ceremony of descent
of flesh into cupola of flesh,
yet unwilling to discriminate
in what is thrust and what is grasp.

Perplexing: indenture of what
was made to grasp, absorb, as
tearing-off and tearing-out
are process of exchange — detritus
of spent affection: ravening
head and watery cusp; collusion;
journeying in trust, lever and
levering combine their singularities.

So rudimentary thrust and swell
must, in mutual ardour, spell
what God in nature most demands,
that female in her nature stands
for insertion, her delight
in taking into darkness light
as from her innards to expel
a further denizen of hell.

So, tortured by this contradiction
of priming good things with extinction,
man labours hard to make much sense
why cock and balls are so immense
as first in foetus swift to grow
when all that coming has to show
is pain and more pain in arrears
until the outcome disappears

– which cause, begun with such delight,
ends in everlasting night.

She

The silence fakes.
          She tremors still.
Still tremors. Shakes.
          The coming ill,
ill coming: quakes.

          All night she has been
dreaming.
          In the dawn
she waits —
          the turbulence, the drive;
the coming still
          that never makes
the going brighter
          that she shakes,
shudders
          to such
artificial means
          and bends.

Shadows and re-shadows from a single light
measure and re-measure my delight
as body turns and angel cries
— the light reflected in her eyes —
the servility of loving less
that, nightly, in her loving, she denies.

Our Room

The clock ticks on in the evening room,
between extremes of joy and gloom.

Now sleeps this cushioned breast
      and arm,
laid in inoffensive charm
      across the fold of pillow, pressed
where, in such display,
      undressed,
you lay,
      half-yawning, half-reclined.
(Covert body, covert mind.)
      In such display
to me inclined –
      temporal: just. Ecstatic – quite,
loving in such move and more despite
      our hours subtracted from the street outside
– the rush of traffic, crowd and world
      to pride
in flesh and gesture, whirled
      to where, in this bed, as in respite,
we tame our love to love at sight:
      sweet-natured lyer by my hand,
in you, may I such love command?

Passion

Strange, how passion sits
     in the tormented: subsides
     expires, sleeps, qualifies
        its distance in repose:
seeks nothing but its aimless rise
     in its persecuted's eyes,
fired by what it rouses most.

She waits, sleeps in civility and lies
     along the tendon of his thigh,
tempered to a kiss:
     how circumspect she is,
victim of her victim's charm,
     victim of his own alarm.
Nothing rests: his tempers rise,
     his feeling nothing to the crime
of burning in his own desire, desirous
     of her universe.

Great Love

The great loves
        that the lover dies on
leaving one behind
        one foot in the grave
the other
        poised in ungravitated
time:
        moved sensationally
by what is left behind
        and lost
and what is lost
        yet stays.

What species of feeling
        does this provoke?
Omission,
        absence more naked
than
        a presence:
everything is here
        — a sound more crystal
than the voice once heard,
        a touch more catastrophic
and complete
        than the feel that came
with hand or foot
        caressing sensationally
the empty air.

Leaving

We sit here
and measure — how far, how near,
how much we move or
have moved, how far
we have to go:
this making-do,
this letting-out
to gauge how much we ought
to leave, where
we will start,
as if, in sitting here,
we measure, endlessly,
how soon we will depart.

III

VOYAGING

Ante-bellum

The air is cooler:
        a breeze blows
from the east:
        a prussian blue
darkens to where the night comes
on. War
has been declared:
this morning, fires: a curfew
allowing us to listen.
We wait.
We are waiting for the silence to resume,
then for the silence to consume
what, all day, in silence, we have listened to.

Bellum

It's all a sham,
this world where wisdom
        first began:
there's nothing
here for beast or man
            to justify this suffering.

War is always with us, war is:
this is what war is, is this:
bomb and bullet, blood and gore
(all we knew, in fact, before):
this is what war is, is this,
this is what war is:

to give some other bastard hell,
assuring him and you as well
that war as war is always true
to all that war as war can do.

All that peace as peace can bring
is restlessness that it begin
another bout of action, friend:
o be my foe that we may end
all that peace as peace can do
to make me wish that I were you.

War is always with us, war is,
this is what war is, is this:
bomb and bullet, blood and gore
(all we knew, in fact, before);
this is what war is, is this,
this is what war is:

to kill poor bastards by the score
(that is what our war is for):
to kill before each bastard shout
help, or peace, or I surrender:
nothing in our lives is kinder
to those who seek an end to doubt.

Friend, o friend, do not despair,
finality and death are here:
this is what our nature wanted,
this is what our nature vaunted:
this is true of nature raw:
all that nature wants is war.

War is always with us, war is.
This is what war is, is this:
blood, not kisses, rape, not wife
to fuck in bed throughout your life:
this is what war is, is this,
this is what war is.

Like autumn and the mists and fruit,
the impulse to become a brute
is true to nature's ordering
as lion cast as nature's king.
How consistent we have been
to all that God as God has seen

contentedly as his first plan
for man to be a beast to man
(from his perception to uphold
not what is weak but what is bold),
as bird off worm and dog off flea
to the end of God's eternity.

This is what war is, is this,
this is what war is:
> *no problem or unease*
> *but doing what you please*
> *to batter, splat and screw:*
> *that's what we're here to do:*

that's how God's venture first began
to hand God's nature on to man.
Our nature must, as nature, view
what man as man has got to do,
not only sense but care as well
to make God's heaven ring like hell.

War is with us to the end:
o come, dear foe, and be my friend.
O be my foe, let us endure
what God as God has made us for.

Journeying

Roads similar to this combine
the better their contour to define
– moving to Perplexity, Conjecture, Common Sense:
cities whose destinies commence

to shape our leaving-in and leaving-out,
the arbitrary obfuscation of vivid route
to what, in broader street, becomes a state,
a kingdom ruled by opiate,

whose streets are paved with ash and bone,
where what we loved and knew are shown
as little less than what they are – exceptions,
fortuitous signals of deception –
a way of aloneness to a kingdom we lament:
all roads lead nowhere that lead to our content.

Voyagers

We each take what we can:
      give what we owe
(determined by another's won't);
      pleasure that we lease from pain
count as our loss
      or gain,
changing
      as we give it space,
manoeuvre it to
      what we will or won't.

Our little cargo we invest —
      lay out on quay,
invite demand:
      marry our wish to what we can inspire
in custom:
      take up our penny and our pride
and peddle it
      far off,
or near,
      to brink of time,
to edge where knowing
      and not knowing
coalesce.

                Vast merchant ship comes curling in,
domestic to our breeze
                and blooms,
gracious in its gravity,
                and beams,
harshly,
                by our rocks and shoals.
The merchants and their families go aboard:
                crew, captain, at this berth, are dazed —
they have come home,
                bringing our future with their past,
farers of the mind and heart,
                hearthless.

At night the ship lies empty:
                everything is stowed:
a lamp burns at the helm,
                shadowing the mast.
Water splutters at the bow:
                the bulbous hulk that on the sea has tossed
is turned. The men have gone,
                some are home,
some on tracks through moonlit wood or field.
                The captain sleeps at the merchant's house.
They are all removed.
                The ship shudders.
Soon, futurity will begin again:
                'See here', and, 'here', and 'here' again —
tapping at a chart:
                'here we will end'.

They have come back.
      What they have seen we will become,
bracing to the swell,
      moving us,
these mariners of intent,
      these merchants of desire,
these voyagers of the heart.

Campaigners

The crowds and traffic filtered by.
      We seldom laughed:
that came from other tables.
      We talked:
we were activists.
      Later,
one of us made bombs,
      another manufactured chairs,
another married –
      not a woman, but another man.
Another painted pictures.
      One killed himself.
Several disappeared.

Strange, looking back, how
living eludes us,
    slipping into the present,
even though we hold it back,
    retain it,
at cafe tables:
    the city darkens overhead,
stars appear,
    windows come alight:
our talk flies from us, our voices
    rise in the evening air:
it is happening,
    all the time —
as elusive as a word, a sign,
    half-acknowledged,
at tables,
    moving beyond us
as if hearing one another
    after each of us has died.

Survivors

I am the demon, the king
     and the clown:
in me congruities meet:
     fatalities
which in our rise sway past:
     'All these have died'.

Survivors,
     we mourn then turn again,
summon the day, forestall the night,
     hurried in our living,
bringing in the light,
     anticipating in their past
the things we have become.

The Prince

We came to the castle:
no one lived there any more:
                            windows empty,
drawbridge down but split apart,
                            the outer bailey and the barbican
deserted.
            The earth, grassless, was strewn
with dung.
            The drawbridge to the keep was up.
The moat was dry.
            Birds flew out of windows.
An animal
            scurried from a door.
            I caught a glimpse of colour:
a rag
            fluttered, high up,
                            from a broken stair.

From here the king, in the midst of his courtiers,
                            had ridden out.
Betrayed,
            cut off from the castle,
                            he had fled —
caught at the door of the Chapel
standing on the nine-arched bridge
                            leading to the town.

His head, spiked, had been displayed with others:
carrion ripped out his eyes and brain.

So much for miscalculation, when
                              the enemy without the gates
is fortified by the confidence within.
I imagined the spike behind my tongue,
the carrion beak inside my eye,
my brain sucked down the ravenous throat.

Already the stone was being used:
                              walls,
a bridge, half-destroyed by the betraying horde.
In years the castle, too, would be destroyed:
                              festooned with weed:
the eye-socket of the dead king's skull
would be like the window of his keep.
'Time, the great dispenser', I was told.

The castle stands upon a hill:
a river, below, runs to the Chantry Bridge.
The Chantry Bridge leads to the town.
I will pray in the chapel.
I shall ride away.
That way they will never know who I really am.
Who my progeny are.
          Where they are.
What they will do.
          What they have become.
By saying nothing I shall keep my peace.

Time does not dispense: it focuses,
          intensifies,
makes things like steel,
          laying out the past in the days that are to come.

Faith

Ours is a medieval city:
　　　towers, domes, steeples —
thoroughfares of cobbled stone:
　　　alleyways run between the buildings,
opening into yards.

　　　Roads wind off across the hills.
At the backs of the yards, behind the houses,
　　　are the brick-walled gardens.
Fountains play on moss-strewn lawns.

　　　A river is crossed by a nine-arched bridge,
the central arch extended
　　　by a prow-shaped chapel around which
the rock-strewn water flows.

　　　The people are busy:
carts grind against the cobble.
　　　Choirs rise against the noise of bells and birds.
Long after we are gone
　　　this place will be no more:

out of that dust fortuity again may rise
　　　in the shape of city walls,
dust harbouring dust,
　　　each gram and grain of us
as old as something new.

Paid-off

You would not know
the pits are here:
the dynamos, headgears,
gantries, tracks. It is near
what it was before:

sculptors
have overcome the old inversion
of the pits — Crigglestone,
Walton,
Roundwood, Manor:

no more
remembered than
a state of mind,
a vacuity that these infillings
swell, leaving

their imprint,
an influx of the dead
(colliers of intent).
How little they deface
what they replaced:

earthiness,
greatness,
a thousand
roadways, consignment
of stale air —

those gougings-out go
unattended in these
pits which no
one but us
would know were there.

Pit

Still this waiting
      where we descend in
each successive pit,
      collecting what
is buried, what
      we have found. Impasse:
where flesh
      and bone, senses
and the like, no more
      survive than in these
depths can you or
      I outlast what
we descended through.
      We listen, crave what
first we found,
      this evenness,
this temperateness,
      this moving into what
we know, here, looking upward
      into blacknesses
and downwards
      into light.

Time

Life moves in incalculable ways
                                its wonders to endorse:
gives rise to some before their fall
(gives fall to others at their rise),
while others fall and never stop,
drop succeeding drop
                                (into the pitiless pit of time).

Life gives consistency a better name
(nothing so prevalent as distress):
nothing lasts that does not last for ill:
time, the great achiever, posts its bill
with a regularity which time and death alone endorse,
the one convener, the other, subject force;
while we agree time takes its time
                                and times it right,
sole arbiter of reason, shade and light –
                                sole occupant of space as well –
as conjurer made captive to his captive spell
so time times time, they say, in hell.

Reality

Shit is life
and life is shit:
that is all ye need to know
before you're hit by it.

Hope is retrospective:
it flies
            in face of reason;
despair prospective —
it comes in
            in season —

sure as Fall or May,
or night that follows day:
so blackness is the right
by which we measure light
and watch it fade away.

The suffering we ignore
(and place outside the door —
until it shoulders in)
is like the need for sin
to hasten those intent
on wishing to relent:
so blackness in the guise
of wisdom to the wise
is equal to the hope
that is wisdom to the dope.

Preparing for the worst
is how our life is cursed:
it never is as bad —
it's always something worse.

So said the man who came
to check our broken drain
(consumed, he said, by his confession
shit something now of a profession).

But what he sensed no doubt was true
(looking from the drain to you),
that what is hope and what is love
survive amidst the shit, my dove.

Philosophy

He valued screwing up his life
(it was with that impulse that he took a wife):
from his conception to his end
all life had asked was he pretend
to meaning
in his madness as
madness in his
not pretending.
The statistical three score years and ten
were therefore there to time exactly when
everything, he'd prove, would have a cause —
to which effect he offered pause
for it to show itself, and yet
no explanation in that time had set
his mind or feelings at their ease:
pain, madness, terror and the like
were there because and not despite
the fact that life, like death, was a disease.

Second Chance

When his children
        left he picked another:
(his wife, by now, was
        simply 'mother').
A child and bride he chose
        as one:
(to call her, in her absence, 'lover').

He took a cold, hard stance
        (in face of remonstrance),
and taught his lover how to dance,
        took holidays in France
(that kind of dull romance)
        — 'Not bad,' as he put it, 'in the circumstance' —
not merely his last but second chance.

That, Too

Dying,
   looked at his hand:
his thumb-nail
   cracked.
That, too.

Left finger, scarred:
   yes:
veined like a leaf,
   tubular within.
That, too.

Diagonally below,
   the garden:
pale blue,
   deep red,
magenta:
   variegated green of leaf
and grass,
   flecked through and through.
That, too.

The noise of bells,
 blown by a breeze
from an open window across the backs
 images the East:
the proverbial philosophic stone
 which,
behind the philosophic back,
 dies too,
unseen
 − still there,
yet gone,
 invisibly,
still there,
 but gone.
That, too.

The Old Conundrum

The old conundrum:
        'a chemo-physiological phenomenon',
'a perturbation of the brain
        due less to circumstance
than gene'.

        Little to be gained from harping after God,
or laying down the blame:
        'the horror of it all'.
That's right:
        this animal creation,
this animal delight,
        crated in a creature that
knows scarcely day from night.

Relapse

Relapse: when we go backwards
into pain and move towards
those endings that we left behind
(better to be cruel than unkind).

Remorseless in our stepping-back
when all in love and life we lack
is kindness, softness and ingress
into sorority and brotherhood to redress

the bloodying cut and crush of time.
Backwards we are content to climb
when forwards obliquity we assume
to be the certain path to doom.

Anxious, analytical, we digress
the better to impress
not friends and others
but our own distress,

annihilating it with backward glance;
in retrogression is our only chance
to circumvent the present,
outlive the past — resent-

ful of what delay we find
in being true to being kind.
(If in our life no error we detect
distaste may still be found at its effect.)

So day by day and night by night
we measure backwards our delight:
in being true to being wrong
we silence what, before, in song

to presence and to present found
in life congruent to a round
of looking at not back or on
the better joy to feed upon.

So in our past our future lies,
while all around us backward eyes
look to what was not but is
to end all our beginnings with remiss;

for past as future we surmise —
what's past re-written with each enterprise
of changing all each time we look
to find good outcome as in book

(to make that reading feel worthwhile
so, fictional, to the past beguile
we as to grave romance
of making past and present dance

to a tune that is endowed
with good intent, as if to shroud
what should be true with false attire
the better our past as present to expire).

If in effect we find no fault
then forwards backwards we can halt
to find in past our one complaint
that made us not what we are but what we ain't.

Intent

I came here when lunatics
were all the fashion:
madness came from home not passion
— from parents, public,
and the like, a sign, not of disturbance
but compliance
to a need
from which all
but the normal
had been freed.

Now they've found it's all in us
coming here is not much fun:
no longer 'symptom of the times' — just
another useless bum.
(Tear my nails out in despair,
mistake my mother for a chair,
not because of what she's done —
I am, she says, her loving son —
but cos they say I'm 'not quite there',
or what I have 'up top' is 'spare'.)

Otherwise I'm getting madder:
no one saying that is sadder,
seeing as what I am is fine
by rules which only I divine.
'Dear friends and brothers,' I begin,
'let us consider God a sin,'
only to be taken in.

No mind is more than its intent:
in comradeship I find content.
God, if he's here, must show his hand
not in what I seem but what I am.
Why else should he come here below
if not to me to nurse to show
his love, forgiveness, and the rest
in hoping — as I do — it's for the best?

Otherwise I'm nuts for nothing,
put — a bauble — in God's stocking,
as if, at Christmas, put in there
to save the bugger from despair
(a little piece of harmless fun:
'What's another useless bum?').
No, no: I'm mad because it reads
'Mad is precisely what God needs.'

Intent

Is there not something here that's wrong,
a note mis-cued, misheard in song,
a guidance that has not gone right,
conductor's signal out of sight,
misread, mislaid, mischieved?

Pain is the parcel that we bring
when, anxious for respite, invited in,
we play the game that gamesters know
in passing pain to pain to show
that all but one can be relieved.

How does this horror further blight
the move of loved one out of sight
when death, disease and madness rise
past fidelity, hope and wise
counselling that love alone achieved?

What can bestow, what can survive
when, caught in web, that web alive
with terror, dread, despair, deceit
that in their turn are in receipt
of love that love alone has grieved?

Remember nothing, save even less,
when measuring life with love's distress:
beyond that love no love can go
into the wildness that was there before
all but love in love perceived.

O reckon nothing, counsel sense,
love, at the end, is but pretence:
live for the day, beyond forget
what terror and all else will let
free the moment love's conceived.

History is but fiction; fictionless
we call and fictionless
invent what we,
in seeing, long to see,
the love of man by God deceived.

If this were true how would we grieve
all that suffered, all that leave
all that love as love can lend –
as love on love, in love, expend
on all that love in life believed?

Our only solace, source and end
is all that this distress can send
past wildness, death itself, and find
in love the love that can unwind
the endlessness of love when love's received.

Night Prayers

Sleep sweeps in: client
state to kingdom yet
to come. Each evening
ring and hear
her voice: this we will
love. All minds
and matter in this
business speak – placed
for her, by her: how
living might be
light, aspiring
to be greater than it
is, or might have
been, or was. Please
her to return.

Thoughts fall hard: such
hardness to resist: say
we are here for
fellowship: no more
departures. No ending
until such ending
come.

Canticle

At least it will happen:
sometime. We wait. Fears
congregate. Say
you love me. 'I live
for nothing', or
'for everything', or, 'for
all', yet all we
live for has
been less than
this. A kiss. Consensus
of our loving would
declare that nothing has
been loved or lived. Fires
play their part: forgetfulness
declares what
lives within
is levered out, free
of our despair.

Night Thoughts

He waits:
    all night he has
drawn sense
    from senselessness,
foretelling
    why and where,
and when and how:
    nothing
in this place
    shapes shade
or light,
    everything obscure,
intending rather
    than expressing.
Soon it will be here,
    the unimaginable,
this portent
    he has been dreaming of.

ii
These strange affairs
     that take place
when the mind is turned
     not to
but from and
     finds in
alter-stare
     the maze of what
all night
     it has been thinking:
the stuff
     of syllogism
or rational suit
     to suave solipsist
in his or her pursuit
     of something
strong in contrast
     to this
something weak yet true.

iii

Recent misconceptions that
     dictate what
might have been or
     almost were or
came about
     as rout
of common sense, the censure
     of irreality
which, by
     its leaving-out,
leaves in
     the necessity of sin.

iv

What features in the mind foretell
how in these streets, these passages,
these houses, congregates the spell
of dreams and dreamsters
(dreamt by us as well):
dreamless sleepers dreamily awake
at early hour when shift of reason bares
what dreamless night itself despairs
of seeing in the dark.

146

v

In the corner where
        the extraordinary
and the able
        have shown
all their
        lives the inhospitable
side and silence
        of their imagining
or slide
        into and out
of what they concede
        their licence
to deceive
        as burglar or assassin
musters or
        selects
slyly
        it is not easy
this
        playing-in of
torment and distress that
        havoc sense
and move
        without remorse
to find when
        all else dies
all dying stops.

vi

How do you take this tattered mind
        that, tortured as it is,
craves guidance, forbearance,
        kindness,
gentleness? This vessel
        ready to obey:

        as mind propounds
        what heart confounds,

        as mind infers
        what heart deters,

        as minds suppress
        what hearts confess,

        for minds oppose
        the heart's repose,

        as wisdom halts
        what heart must fault,

        or woman mind
        what man may find

        in all her gentleness.

The melting and the massacre begin
when all we have to share is sin.

148

Can't

Can't settle on this order which,
in offering more,
        gives even less
than what we had before:
        distress,
confinement and the rest, such
        pain as pain will settle for.

Can't recognise this stance which,
in posing as it does,
        provides
for loser and the lost alike foes
        that loss
itself was privy to, rich
        ending as rich ending goes.

Can't figure out a system which,
no matter how
        it measures or
expands, must show
        more
than it pitch
        deferment to a depth that by
                its depth is hidden so.

Can't reconcile a living which,
by its demise,
        takes
virtue, order by surprise
        and in disease
and madness filch
        what was wisdom from the wise.

Can't govern a principality which
in governance
          alone
eschews
          what governance
itself would use
          if it in charity and wisdom touches
not when devilry and defilement it accuse.

Can't tolerate the terror which,
night and day,
          neither
time nor kindness can delay
          but terror
at the terror retch
          as at a loved one gone astray.

Hell is this which
neither
          love nor hatred can distract
but further
          fear and fury rack
what lunacy itself may fetch
          when pain to no other but itself attract.

Can't release myself from this to which
nothing that we know
        or feel
can, no matter what I do,
        appeal:
a dissonance of light that offers much
        to dissonance alone to steal.

Virgin Birth

Losses and defeats:
        to something other than herself concedes
all that light itself completes:
        long-view of, short-term,
what she can
        decipher in her loving man,
mouse and creature unreleased
        on world despoiled yet still appeased
by what she catches
        from each breath and burst
of what she touches.

Deciphers in the tea
        leaves or span of cards
what life is taking her towards
        – backwards into death
or worse –
        how
nothing but her pride
        can give her
something precious she can hide –
        her pain,
her lying-low.

Long-lover of her relatives,
        deceased,
no love in life or life in love released
        but into pitch and tossing
of distress,
        that anguished tethering to mate
or less
        in concubinage ceased.

Possesses now each day anew
        in torment, at her state, to view
what animal as man can do
        — defile and bugger and befoul
in vilest venture screw
        what all life-long, to her, was precious,
new
        to woman's own creation.

Not something that she seeks,
        sensation,
at all that in the vilest can
        daily, in its issue, ram
vileness into worse,
        no more than she endorse
or curse
        that, in the worst of all worlds,
this is the worst.

Animal to animal
        can not, in this displeasure,
more than man to woman measure
        daily in its drive to prove
that what is needed is not love
        but guile
to covet earth a while
        before its final ending.

Can she conserve
        what from this vileness she extracts,
the love that loveliness attracts,
        the love that she deserves,
the worth
        that love alone
is mending
        on her own polluted earth?

If, on the evening, she subsides
        and to her pillow as to friend confides
what all night long and day she feels
        (the death-in-life from which she steals),
in bed and bed alone submits
        to touchless, taintless sheet and sighs,
and to herself alone admits
        what to herself alone she cries:

        'A woman by her God deceived:
        a monster in her womb conceived!'

IV

THE DANCING DOG

Composition

Cold comes in the window tonight,
and rain. Spattering on the floor, it stains
the wood, the carpet edge, the light
catching as it falls the rain's
flecked lash and litter, darkening here
as footfalls, casual, irregular, spaced
carelessly about the floor where
paper curls and shakes, each faced
sheet symmetrical with ink
sinking out in smudge and flare
as if each damp fleck to link
to other spattering to share,
in new imprint of message, rash
information from the elements of wind
and rain outside, and dark, fresh
inswill from the night to bind
such peregrinations that the mind might
move or be moved to by this casual
intrusion. Another light
to shine in a familiar dark, unusual
signature and sign of greeting
as if to re-compose or introduce
what mattered on each page when writing
first-ordered patterns in the truce
of one thought conflicted with another,
feeling with feeling, disposition of sense
and place, of time, and that otherwise inexpressible offence
that raises order from an order known
and in fresh conjugation of familiar effect
makes unfamiliar what has grown

unhindered to be true and not defect:
true, that is, of mark that marks as if in song
what right, in this, may wrest from wrong.

Posterity

We'll leave these children when we go
– marks painted on a domino:
evidence of their number – four,
of symmetry and unison, our
message that we loved in kind
as parents of our parents left behind
in their small trace
of love or less the grace
of their own living. So we go:
one more signal to
the edge of time
as each, in turn, their signal sends
to where this message ends
in the senselessness of rhythm, pattern, rhyme.

Pause

Commemorate each visit
as we do by sitting at the window
late at night:
the haul of wave
across the shore:
the resuscitation, as by sound,
of wind and shale,
a dull, harsh scrawl,
one message on another. The Channel
eases its way along the cliff. Cloud,
underlit by towns
along the coast, slides
to a dark horizon. Ships,
at anchor, swing in the division
between sea and cloud.

The estuary, curtailed by roofs,
winds off into the land, water
divining, in reflection, the slow,
uncomplicated addition that
the stream makes to the sea,
a rippled flow round boats
and buoys. Night birds
call as the waves
inswill at the river
mouth. The air is still.

Between us exists a love
of forty years, fettered
by our coming here, to witness
this mirror to our
domesticity, a hotel
room above the sea. We
bind those freedoms marriage
gave: pain shared is
halved. We wait — the
draw of water on
the land, the osculation of
sea across the beach: a
white excrescence crashes
down to bring in
from the darkness
something we have thought
or seen. We wait. The
sea-cry of the birds
returns from the sand-banks at
the river's mouth — into
a room that reflects
the part that
darkness plays around and
with our arbitrary light. Sounds
echo up the slope
behind. We have been coming
here for twenty years:

in the night-sail
of a boat processing from
the river-mouth I visualise
a father's spirit returning
to the sea he loved and
sailed and spoke of all
his life. I visualise
our witness passing here, waiting
for the cry of birds, for
the slow expulsion
of the sea as it
tires against the land — waiting
for our lives to rise, to
present themselves, freshly
— for what we value to
remain, our past to
be transformed, like the
moving of the water, westward,
past the sentinels of the
cities' lamps — the
slow levering of change against
the endless shifting.

Children

Child crying in the backs tonight
calls up the crying in our past
when, from the bed, we heard
the children
roused by pain, discomfort, dream,
call in distress that drew us on
to merely what we had become:
joint-holders of this child-predicament
which, wretched in those early hours,
roused us as bearers of a gift ourselves,
returning self to self as if endowed
with god-like suspension of time and place,
stretching our longevity beyond the grave:
we die and, dying, know that we are saved.

Child

Eyes closed,
          pale lashes flicker,
thumb suckled in his mouth,
          this offspring of our offspring,
part-parcelled from another world,
          this federation
of pale skin, blond hair
          (eyes blue beneath the flickered lids).
What does he owe us?
          The dissonance of thought,
or worse,
          fraught feeling,
dissemblement,
          of living by a truth we curse.

ii

Strange, moving out of dark to light,
to see how ends meet means still out of sight:

fair-featured angel in its cot
          counts less
each moment that it moves:
          a long subtraction
from its past,
          diverting present,
forestalling yet-to-come —
          the will to see each flicker out:
a system of beliefs that says,
          though sum is added,
nothing counts.

If nothing counts
　　　how does the count begin
that counts as nothing
　　　the good that counts as sin?

iii
System of betrayal,
　　　the test to truth and sin:
all roads that lead to hell,
　　　I'm told, are roads that lead within.

Don't know, in truth, where truth begins:
　　　if scarcely in our goodness then
more surely in our sins.

iv
Intractable, this problem
　　　of being two in one:
one dead within,
　　　one living out:
one hauling up,
　　　one hauling down:
dissemblement
　　　of how and why
as if,
　　　in craving how to live,
we are asking how to die.

Visiting

Yesterday drove down
to see a daughter in
her new house, refurbished
by herself and partner: walked
by the river
after lunch, carrying her
child: the unison of unblended
parts subsumed
in song
and dance, jogging on
my shoulder,
he treasured
as the cargo that I
carry from the past, my
voyage almost done, his
started to discovery and loss:
the wastes that move him to our
path until we share
with him a forward sight
into a dark transfigured by his light.

The Visit

We walked by the river
        talking of
what makes things go,
        what holds them back:
a father and his daughter —
        a daughter's child
pushed sleeping in its pram
        before us on the rivered track.

We talked of love
        and its demise:
of what was strong
        and fevered and extreme
now faded and discarded,
        old and wrong.

How could it go,
        how could it come
unlooked for? love
        natural as the breath
of grandchild
        sleeping in its pram,
its pouting face, its long-lashed eyes,
        the product of such enterprise
as love gets down to
        in tenderness and pity.

We talked of rowing
        (scullers in the evening
air creaking their way to a distant lock);
        of war,
of family life
        (long-past in our case, now, in hers, begun);
of parental poise
        (of games and family plays
and long-remembered toys).
        The river darkened.
Sounds lengthened in the dusk.

We talked once more of love,
      as if we might invent
a new parabola
      for its descent. Yet
love survives,
      I thought,
in sleeping child
      placed in its pram
as in a dream,
      things really in that way
as they may seem
      at sudden glance
— an angel sleeping in a trance,
      pleasure in its hidden eyes
not hurt
      hurled to where
darkness beckons light,
      good there
as if to measure bad,
      light darkness
gladness pain.

        We wandered on.
Pram
        shuddered at the path;
the eyes of grandchild
        turned,
saw the mother face
        and closed.
When, in repose, it sees again
        may it this moment love recall
the better its own darkness to dispel
        and in such move its lightness prove
as child to parent
        it once more propel.

Adam and Eve

This music is a pretext for
dissemblement: nothing
we give do we impart
without that prejudice
which grows more
closely to us,
wearing truth and trust away
— as if such counter to our delight
is to turn each love
and longing
into night.
(Such sight
and strain
do we refrain
from entering
in our train
of seeing
what we need or mean
to entertain.)

Such wisdom that we covet in repose
declines to keep us
wise or cool in
our enterprise to find
what, when we go,
we leave behind
in gesture, sign or
chance. How temporal
it all
is,
the cicatrical
texture, the shaping
of each hand, each nail: nothing
lasts: each integument that quarters
muscle,
bone, blood, orifice
and else
means less and less
until such pain
has hollowed out all that came in
in yearning,
persuasion: nothing
is left out or in
– or something is:
a nothingness prevails
where nothing is
defining something was
or will be or might come again.

Let's feel it here,
let's be it here,
here where
this waiting,
this expulsion, this dying
now begin.

The Dancing Dog

The light across
the estuary fades, dies
on the shoals at the river
mouth, widening
to the clouds and cities
down the coast. The air
is moving
from the sea, bringing in
the cry of birds and
the voice of a stroller on the sand,
a dog marooned among
the dunes. It brings
a presage of the south,
the move of warmth
as, here, you stir
to the shifting in
the light of shafted clouds
– the opalescent glow or
tortured wound –
flanged edge of flame around
a setting sun. This evening
is our coming-to, our rousing
from the doldrum of the year,
the resurgence of your
parent to her
death. We have seen this estuary
before, the caverning
grip of hills, a thousand murmurings
that come in with the wind:
this, our confessional
not of truth but fear,

this burning at hell's
mouth, fingering our
glowing faces here,
fingering the stroller
walking on the shore, sending
his shadow up the sand
to the prancing
figure of a dancing
dog.

      We have danced our
days away, danced in our
youth, danced in those
ballrooms where we first saw
the visaged bandsman dancing
down the years: the drive in
and onward of the waning
light. Nothing
can accustom us,
nor this, to what is here,
the light in the stranded
shoals at the river mouth, stronger
than the sky itself, the indifference
that strengthens when neither
you nor dying parent
will be here,
poised at this window,
turning in the light in this, our
carousel of fear.

Pain

Remission, and returning to
suspicion of his past:
the plight of what he'd laboured from,
to a light he'd meant to last.

Pain — and stricter
pain to bear: sharp censor
of the pain's redress,
the better always to assess

what pain as pain's intended for:
to help, to hinder, or
reveal the final stricture
death or worse, the picture

framed
by pain itself, sustained,
unending, caught
as pain to other pain is brought,

mind wearied by all
mind subject to: the fall
from grace that birth commends
goes on as fall that never ends,

the catastrophe that merely brings
the goodness that as goodness sins
that we may know salvation
solely as the prelude to damnation

(as if our darkness to declare
that hope is prelude to despair).
Cast this aside, what do we find
but sight as anger of the blind,

sound of the deaf, speech
of the dumb? reach
for our pain as for the sum
of all the ways we have to run,

from darkness into darker still
as if our pleasure to fulfil
God's misconception of delight
in ending all our days in night.

(Earth knows no greater pleasure than
to hand God's turmoil on to man.)
Such pain, as pain, that we abhor
is what we were intended for:

feel this, feel that, feel nothing less —
pain is our paean of distress.
First breath, first pain,
and then we rise,

God's purpose plain
in creatures' eyes:
to find in death our final gain
that what our God requires is pain.

Non Sequitur

Know all or nothing in our track
      from death to life and back,
our living message of a kind
      as to a runner
handing on to other
      in a race begun before his time.

Odd, this handing-on
                as mother-daughter, father-son,
sustained by pace alone
                at times, unquestioning
of our chance of moving
                in our life to death,
of summoning pain
                as if to stress
that punishment is gain
                or is our redress
for being in the first place
                so engaged. Race
slow or fast,
                decline or rise,
this is the strangest enterprise
                of running to our death as
if born only to be sacrificed,
                the bearer of a message
whose language
                and intent we never
learn, as if, a courier,
                we must face the challenge
of not knowing, or,
                falling as we die,
not asking, 'Why?'

Death-zone

I've moved to the death-zone
        now:
most of my contemporaries already
        are.
I, through them, have super-
        ceded
what they, in dying,
        lost.
At what cost. Through
        them
I have acquired
        what they desired
(non-mimic view
        of mimic world),
into reality,
        step
by backward step
        hurled
as emissary. All
        the better
to be without intent
        or
displeasure at our discontent,
        restless
as the monarch
        we abjure,
the penurious
        dissembler,
life's pretender,
        cured of pride
by rapid fall,

        the better our distress to
call,
        'Marvellous!' 'Intended!'
Nothing
        in our lives
did we refuse,
        dying
as we moved until
        we found
what mattered most:
        doing what had not been done,
        seeking what had not been sought.

Poor buggers:
        their minds, for
most part,
        not interned
on edge
        of crisis:
wisdom
        of a kind
they lent: parabolas
        to measure
their decline. Blind
        to light. In
darkness sought
        a kingdom
of romance: the incredible,
        the unaccountable. Fine
in their darkness
        now. The dark:

that, too, is my delight,
        that tells
that all we choose
        are different hells.
System
        in their suffering, then,
which still defines what
        'gone before' must
surely mean. I dedicate
        what's left: the soldiers
of disparity
        shifting
to the space where no one else has
        gone,
space
        turning
into place, place
        into sanctuary.

Contemporaries

They go,
not even singly,
in these dawn fires
that sleep is strange
in making
rousters, wakeners
— as if obituaries
are our morning's
muse. Fear
and its parent
visibly reside
where friendship
chose to hide.
Life, o life,
to leave such loves,
sovereign and new,
in canvassing not air,
nor light, but shade.

Leaving

Content on leaving
my contemporaries go
with little or no
warning. As in
a play divided up in
parts which no one
has a chance
of learning:

the muttered sense
of what is
left, a memoried
embrace,
a nameless part
that signals silence,
presumption, ambivalence
– the heart.

Mothered

Centred on his helplessness
he lies,
sacred with disease,
trying beyond endurance
to reach what this
might mean. What

quaint position
his body takes, curled
to my mother who sits
decorous with her
ailments nowhere
in his reach, privy
to his privacy. He

dwelt on
words like 'peace':
'I am at peace', and
'pain'
and 'well': for never
fareing did so well as
this misfortune
in his smile, asperity
in his discontent:
to be mothered at his death,
mothered into obliquity,
mothered into silence,
mothered to where his nothing is.

On His Mistress's Death

Came in,
his love,
as in a room:
the letter
said
she'd died last month:
she had 'sent her love
and said goodbye'.
All life is a fantasy:
we create illusions,
call them love':
('Pray, sing to me,' he said, 'my dove':
she singing in a light,
contraltic voice
a song from her audition:
music by Chopin,
if only she had known.)

Yet she came in
as in a room:
'warm and comforting', she said
as when
she smiled
the first time he said,
'I love you.'

He saw the dead more clearly than before,
prefigured in their real world more than his:
a somnambulistic trance –
this time,
his father in his work-time clothes
standing at the door
and, in each successive visit,
younger than before,
passing, in all the cycles of his death,
from coffin shroud to nursery shawl
(a baby in a sea-green chest):
'This is me,
the first Christmas of the century.'

Uncles, brother, father: Lee –
(the sardonic New York face and smile:
'*All life is a fantasy,*' she said:
'*We create illusions, call them love.*'
'*Pray, sing to me,*' he said, '*my dove.*'

Reg, Gilbert, Neville, Father, Lee:
in my swift journey gladden me.

iii

Nothing matters
now
but writing this:
living as a way of death,
caught, the act of dying, on each breath,
less a somnambulistic dance,
the semblance of a trance
(the dead more real than living):
the accumulated force of
what was once considered,
thought of,
done,
then passed.

Nothing matters more than this,
a disentombment
marking
how the dead are still
still
in the movement of the head.

See — the eye;
hear — the ear;
smell — the nostril;
taste — the tongue;
touch — the skin:
the pen and pencil, brush and blade,
solidify the thing within,

reckless as the sensing skin,
tongue, nostril, ear and eye.

Lee

Thinking late: how
you lay in New York,
I in London: you
for 'checks', I for
'cancer': beds in
common.

    'Give him
my love and say
goodbye.'

    Your
apartment looking
down on Third: all-
night traffic thundering
by.

    'Give him
my love and say
goodbye.'

    The
overswinging 'copters,
planes, the symmetrical
space against an
asymmetrical
universe.

    'Give him
my love and say
goodbye.'

Things
change. 'Wouldn't
want it to distress
you.' No.

*'Give him
my love and say
goodbye.'*

Vacillation
between terror,
dread. Savagery.
Can't tell
why it came.

*'Give him
my love and say
goodbye.'*

'Play it
as it comes.' Your
playing-out as if
you saw a semblance
of a chance.

*'Give him
my love and say
goodbye.'*

Generating
in its playing your
sinister demise. 'Play
it with style.'

*'Give him
my love and say
goodbye.'*

No:
my darling, nothing
comes.

Last Moments

Lee, you do not
want to cry, despite
your counselling, your
buddy-in-dying, your
dying to get
well, your figuring
hell, figuring who
is there, where we
are. We are
leaving in a
while. Let us
go in, my love.
Our love, my dear, is
in our parting.

Calm

There is peace here: comes
in each night. Leave
out the calendar
of dying. Death is
counting: leaves
little till the soldiering
in, coming in as
drift, coming in
as guest. Such
knowing. We
change. Behind it
all less knowing
why. Little to
detain us yet
everything to restrain
us, knowing less the
more we learn in
loving we
love everything.

Friend, My Friend

My friend is aged:
    I knew her in her prime.
We shared our youth:
    something of the same ambitions.
We shared ourselves.
    Split whatever there was inside.
(Had our affairs.)

    What bits were left
we gathered to us —
    not much:
those artistries we practised
    in our youth
are gone:
    we traversed time as we might a rock,
displaced by the inscrutable facade
    which marked
and mellowed us.

    A scapegoat, time, I'm told:
a substitute for ills and don'ts:
    negativity accrues
around the thought of something new:
    nothing as present as it seems,
nothing as dreamless, fear
    dying into dream
the moment it arrives.

Old Ones

It was true in those days:
     everything was possible.
In the squares,
     on the lawns,
          each summer,
we talked,
     fashioning, invisibly, what lay around us.
We never faltered:
     thought blanched
          beside the proclivity of things to come.

Now we sit dishevelled,
     not grieving: no.
We tried;
     we made amends:
          we compromised.
Nothing is as easy as it looks.
     We tried harder than we thought we could,
circling the present,
     circumscribing the future,
          honed to the past.

Now, as on those summer lawns,
     we lie,
laid not in groups, as then, but rows,
     equally ambitious,
          turning home,
certain at last
     of what we will become.

Early Love

Those dusty tracks
down which we moved
in Kinsley, Fitzwilliam,
High Ackworth: the ferned
moors between pit dams: no
other place to go
– the slow
turning of our love
to contrive from these
old places our final
ceremony of withholding.

ii
Picture us, stymied
at the start
where pictures hinder
the viewer
from perceiving where
the hand might move,
sharing in the dusk
those strange, ancestral
ceremonies that moved
our fathers: paradisiacal
withholdings, directing
our steps to
where one ill-fashioned
man and one good-
natured woman moved
ceremonially to
congress in a bed.

iii
Those multiple divisions
invisible to the
eye, conjectures
that satisfy not what
is longed for but
despatched: the
moving of pain at
each successive
wakening, wakening to
appal: time after
time we fall to
find that apathy
refuses to
measure anything
at all. How

those quaint seasons
move to our distract,
shaping our discontent,
moving to foretell that
nothing stirs
in our descent, nor
better sense that calls
on one love to
discount the last.

We shape the inept,
design the ill-intent,
ignore the watching.
One grain: we canvass
what we can.

iv

Sovereign we stand
in these, our early pictures,
frozen in our youth, enraptured
by all we knew: entrapped. A
timeless sea moves in behind,
a timeless sky shapes in
the head: a smile trains
on an ageless lens. We
gravitate to people that
we never knew, taking
sky and ocean with us, and
those figments that stand
smiling in the road
behind. These are
what we founded: these
youths that take us
on to where we are, marrying
into the absences of
where we first began.

Late Love

Place feelings side by side.
What was old returns in new.
The latch looses.
Have faith. The detritus
that leaves
leaves us
behind.

Re-settles all
to leave in this
burnt shell
the matrix:
to revive each singular
and distinct effect
to clarify a tender
tumult, summoning
these aches that
fade — wind tremoring.

Wakefield in its summer air
was not the place where
mysteries like these were
first surmised beneath
the St John's sandstone,
these imperfections,
these waves, surfacing in town
(the antiphonal refrain
that quivers to complain:
the sort disorder makes
in facsimile of sense).

Earth moves its cargo less
to show how town shapes
will or city street: what is
lost is not
replaced. Come, rack what's
new and let's devise
this last least
wonder for the wise.

Place feelings side by side.
What was old returns in new.
The latch looses.
Have faith. The detritus
that leaves
leaves us
behind.

Departure

Unwind
each stretch of road:
mounds, not rises,
falls, not hills. Ashes
filter out the sun: crazed
animal, it's said, set
this alight,
turning sand to glass. Wiser
the tread we each
make now, slower
the progress: dimmer
and less safe
the light, sorrow
an antiquated phrase
to leash
to dying. Antiquity of phrase
means more the less
it's shown or used, reminding
what, in moving
on, we leave behind: chapels,
chancels, niches,
absences:
a dispersal
of what we found to last:
the business
of departure. Farewell.
My love. My heart.
As we once more
depart,
leaving, each time, for
our arrival.

Parting

Lovely, the way we part,
sudden, meeting
a resort to being
present when arriving
to depart:
the great farewell with favoured
kiss, to return in new-learned
art.
How swiftly
all these leavings teach, turning
us not from
but to the lesson
we must always learn that loving
each to each is part
of living in each other's heart.

Swift to excise
the murmured line
that pain
is love, each wielder
of a vicious power
that, unceremonious
in its use,
leaves love the victim
of abuse:
wander these rooms
with freedom
to reflect: time slows, quickens —
edges
thought to darker cells where feeling
only to that time defined

what was unbearable,
or bearable,
or uncountenanced,
rift shattered
by an ancient swell of fire
as this slow rage at parting
is withered
by desire.

Return

i
We wait; singularities
combine,
the better their
goodness to define —
retrieve what separation
brought: fellowship,
kinship,
enclosure
of what then
opened out, expanded:
extent of living-in
and living-with
replacing what
was living-out.

ii
No doubts exist:
what was intense
declares
what two years
now have only shown:
how the impossible from
the probable has grown:
more love, more space,
more air, more light,
a surfeit of expansion
in this kingdom of delight.

The old fires
that went with creativity
have gone, replaced by
this inferno here:
no air,
no light,
not even night,
other than what comes
with you. Old loves
dance tamely in the street,
but this configurates
the body and the mind
to dancing of another kind –
to shift irrelevance aside.
Separation
for this while brings home
the sharing that we have in part
and now, together, once more, share
only with the dark.

iv

Searches
and researches
where
to find
his former
convicted state of mind:

shapes
his will
to what he still
remembers
of how he lived without
her loving him about —

less
to redress
what most
in loving would impress:
sensuality,
suavity,

common sense
that other senses
sensed in her
— as his first
rudimentary glance
had turned to stare —

the wholeness,
size, completeness
of seeing in-
to, not from within
this
cornucopia of sin.

v

Listened with care:
what came
to mind
was what had left: 'All
I have suffered', 'All
I have borne'.
She alone
repaid what he had lost.
(He alone
declared what it had cost.)
Life a cage: what he left out
was what she was about.
He canvassed sin there-
fore as to extol what
it might bring —
and so walked in
to take her hand
the better
his story to command.

vi

She's back. This boy
who greets her carried, by
her absence,
to romance.
Shambling,
he comes alone,
waiting
on his own
to find her and not
until that moment move
but
stood his ground to cry,
'So welcome back, my
dear, my love!'

vii
Rests lightly:
conjunction of his opposite
with hers: red hair
with white;
her light
with dark;
the ceremonial
arrival
to report
what she brought
back
(her smile more real until
she and he are indivisible).
All else is lost,
as if he asking how
much she loves when now
he knows how much
it's cost.

viii

His season lifts, celebrating
his decline
into probity, self-censure,
common sense.
Right he was to measure,
canny to withdraw
as to a hilly town in summer,
waking to find
convention in his lying
still, sobriety
in his decline,
levity
in his greeting
here as well
such fiery protégés of hell.

V

THE SAVAGE

Story

No citadel, this spirit, no redoubt
that keeps all but the wrecker out:
the gate and window open wide
on view and antic either side:
regret and misery have gone —
no sound out there, in here, but song —
reclusiveness no longer rules
(this place was once the home of fools):
now kitted out, inside reclaimed
(this refuge of the once-defamed),
it houses no one but the one and only
practitioner of pain and fury,
the poet and painter David Storey.

Poet

Recording his crack-up did
little good:
his system mis-applied to
restoration of recalled intent
as to
what his life
had really meant:
wilderness
of little else
but wife-
encountered mysteries
— sublimities
which in their
time repaid
despatch as balance moved
beyond his care
to support the little that his
sanity could gain
in making from his madness
something of a name.

Artist

I never knew.
      I wasn't told.
It doesn't seem to matter:
      three months gone: death of a son,
not seven years old:
      foetus has a shock as well:
comes out mild
      six months later.
Never cried.

      Quaint spell that dying casts
on bearer and unborn alike:
      grew up, wrote poems,
wrote novels, plays:
      painted pictures,
drew,
      played –
a sedentary serendipity prevailed
      where all else failed,
foiled merely by a discontent
      that came and went
(waking each day to funereal thought:
      death, dying, grief, morbidity, the like),
life governed not by means but ends –
      the foetal castigation: a fortuitous aside –
as if, in prefacing life with death,
      it appended art inside.

Sculptor

He caverned out,
        he shaped,
                he chose:
he marked each element he gave
                to carver, caster,
set rock and stone and metal, wood,
                on plinth,
in natural setting,
                or in whitened room:
flange of stone or steel or bronze,
                armature of wire
flecked upon and shaved,
                caught,
as each a carapace of brain,
                upon, beside, outside
                    his door.

No matter what he made
                or shored,
out of element and dust,
                out of ore and wood,
what mattered most —
                each crest and cranny,
each thrust and rap,
                each boil of ore,
cored as if — the thrill — in poring in
                he poured,
                  gaping
at the mould within.

I Was There

I started painting, so they say, at one:
finger scrawled across a plate.
Wonder what they'd tell me now:
a cicatrical scar, my face:
my eyes look inward, so I'm told, not out.

'Painted pictures as I froze
(painted pictures as I dozed),
painted pictures in my head:
when art was artist's subject chose,
in error, life instead.'

Not much of a hymn to bring back home,
the marching-song of loss and wear,
when caution is the word to use
as, hemmed-in, nations spar with fear.

Far-sighted, find I have no part
of modern ethos' final chart
of who was what and who went where:
all I achieved was, 'I was there.'

Dying Slave

A hammer tapping on a chisel
from the yard below
as might from Michelangelo –
taps, then taps again, an immemorial
roughing-out, a dissertation
as his mind reflects, chips its intent
with metal bit on stone,
the flow of feeling, discontent,
the peregrination of iron
informing an event –
invisible, the source below,
but vivid, furled
as that renaissance hand
moves and, in moving, writes its world.

Women First

Too much done: 'Too much undertaken:
careless with the details
                but not the Grand Design':
what others had failed to do
                or had not imagined,
he would fashion.

He worked on this for forty years:
wondering then on what his life had been about:
                women, mainly,
then offspring.
           When they had left
women entered once again,
           not young, but old,
           older in their ease of life,
who lived for the day,
           the hour,
the time it took for flesh to harbour flesh,
           mortality to rise
           to cheek and breast
in immemorial gentleness.

Delirium

Fear featured strongest,
brought out beneath a cherished
hand in silence; as artist
he declared
what no one previously had aired:

life was a torture,
goodness a pretence,
not source or mover
but despair's defence.

Toyed
with his image, prayed to his dead,
prayed to his loved
ones, prayed to those he had
hardly known:
prayed to the queen,
prayed to the still unread,
prayed to the virgin sheet
that it might spread
involuntarily its own repair
to something still within its care.

(Asked that otherwise silent voice
to measure out in
ink where it had been
— and then rejoice):

or, waited
for that fragment
that might come
when all his other work was done
(finished, had coalesced
in mind-interning idleness).

An Old Sport

'Before the Bartok concerto,' the radio announced,
'we'll play the concerto for violin by Kenneth Leighton.'

I remember him at school:
                    fine hands, fine nose and ears:
the only one excused from games,
                    delicacy evident in his features
— set invariably in profile as,
                    at Assembly,
he played a piece by one of those strange,
                    romantic,
                        luminary
                          figures
who died of T.B.,
             or love,
                or fame
— or a piece composed
             by Ken himself.
Glad to have known him.

In my brussen, competitive, *sporting* way,
I, too, could have done with the same excuse,
                    afternoons with frozen bum,
falling, with a bunch of berks, on rock-hard earth
                  'to do us good'
— etherealising, far better,
                states of mind
                    that,
waylaid by games,
           came roaring in
                when

the games were done.

I'm still here,
            haunted by my disposition to non-aesthetical
pursuits:
punch-drunk from football, cricket,
                            numb, fog-bound afternoons
– liquor, too, can be a problem,
                            and
'fornication by neglect',
                as my second wife
                            before her third
                                    divorce
described it:
            and pills –
                none that characterised
the lives of famous men,
                but pills
that pick you up,
            or put you down:
                    pills
I never needed
            on mud-soaked afternoons,
in drizzle, fog, or snow, or rain
            pounding the pitch with –
                            as it happened
(that sort of game) –
            twenty-nine other pill-less jerks –
            pills

that ease my tired
                    brain,
inhibiting a fear
                    that took the better part
                                        of forty years
to find its full expression
                    here,
            in this gameless, ill-lit,
                                unhealthy room.

A violin
        takes me back along the years
to where the now-dead Leighton
                            with his ungamed
                                    hands
played — how did he describe it?
                    someone's Serenade,
moving me to tears which
                    hidden then,
are all I have to show:
                    terror,
                    dread,
                    paradoxical ill-health:
the fear that each player
                    moves to
when he plays only
            for himself.

What Else Is There?

What else is there
         to celebrate?
         Axiomatic actions,
states of mind
         appropriate to each age:
         in childhood –
terror and delight;
         in youth –
         experimentation.
After that comes
         habit
         disproportionate to the things it guys.

What is this, then,
         when job, wife and children,
         home and car
have gone?
         When children beget children
and familiarity
         passes from the place each night
– to leave
         freedom to re-assess
         or to excite
the family friend who came to tea
         and who
part-sufferer of those ancient days
         commiserates with easy lays,
generous and long
         and full of art
in bedrooms where children
         no longer play a part.

As for the rest —
            senility,
            decay,
before inconsequence is put away
            and all else we thought
            or might have done
exhaled
            — a final breath
anticipating that other common habit, death.

Space To Live

What else?
   Space to move and think:
(a couple of rooms at most,
      with w.c., bath., kit., and g.c.h.,
– could do without the latter at a pinch).
       Not too much disturbance
from either side,
    from overhead
       or underneath –
a couple of windows
     to see, if not a tree,
a patch of grass,
    a road,
frequented at intervals.
    Other than that
      my shelf of pills.

'Nothing has purpose':
      the only positive thing to say
when negativity has its way
       and the nightmare of the day
    is followed
by the terror of the night –
    not dreams and ghoulies
but
   things
which age,
   I would have thought,
should have put beyond the pale:
       uncertainty
       and doubt

which bed., kit., bath., mod.cons., and g.c.h., et al,
are incapable of keeping out.

B.J.

A friend of thirty years:
               B.J.
          'A giant of the modern age'
(described in one of last week's Sunday papers):
all he's made, throughout his life, are 'filums'.
Not sure about his age:
               a 'prodigal talent' in his early days
('a colossus' now), 'a seminal source'.
Of what?
          Not sure:
nor ever, quite, what 'makes him tick':
a 'pyknic' figure,
baggy 'trews', red shirt,
grey-haired
               (a reef, the wisps, around his omphalotic skull):
short-armed
(no wife and kids):
not clinical, yet undetached
(cerebral yet sentimental):
a still-surviving Galway voice:
'Filums are', says he, 'the medium of the age.
Ours is the age of filums, friend.'

Uncertain, as I listen, what he means:
                         no screen or camera
transposes what goes on
                    inside my head.
I flick through old discrepancies
                    and doubts
that blot the visual image out
                    and wing their way to a consciousness

I scarcely thought
          or knew about.

'Filums' may be accessible,
               or artily obscure,
yet scarcely resonate to where old Homer learned his line,
or Solomon scrawled his signature of love.

Legislators, scarcely, of our own affairs,
irrelevant us rhymesters now,
testifiers to a fashion that passed
                    when cameras
and the like
      began
to note
the — how should I describe it? —
               phaticity of man.

Bard

Little to declare, little to extol,
      the cornucopia of feeling full,
antiphonal to his despair,
      a species of illegal fare
favoured to his temperament or
      fairing to his nature.

Sanguine and remote, sole arbiter
      between his desk and door,
this seminal track that led him
      on to what propriety might find –
the one-eyed beggar in
      the kingdom of the blind:

the lattice window, fireplace, desk,
      the brow perusing Holinshed
or Plautus; the candle-flicker
      on the wall. Flames crackle
round a log. The floorboard creaks.
      A residue of noise comes from the street,

the footsteps dull on stone and cobble.
      There is little evidence of books.
He thinks: the melancholic stare of a mono-
      syllabic comedian who in his 'yes' and 'no'
counters speculation in the bony scrape of ink:
      the scrawl that runs in active then in

passive line, quivers, each rustle
        followed by his dark-pupilled gaze,
as if the shaven bone and vegetable dye
        eradicate what the luminescent eye
is thinking still: the features
        of a listener.

He lifts his head: the buttressed
        wall, the uneven line of timbered
floor, the ingress of a draught
        that flickers at the fire.
He gazes at the street:
        the encroaching opposite

house, a facade where a reciprocal
        glow moves behind a similar
pane: his eyes move down.
        The quill spills on
in patterned, horizontal
        scrape, each indenture

of thought, of finger
        poised on pen, quivering
as each word-line runs from the body
        to a half-contented eye
reflecting what that hand effortlessly
        subscribes to. He ruminates

on that blankness
        beyond his final mark — caresses
the ink with quill-point: draws
        out the blot to the features
of a face. The ink-darkened tissue
        moves again. What is this

moment when fluidity
        distills its skill reflexively
upon a watered pulp, dyeing
        its way into this reflexive
space — to encapsulate in that domed head
        and tapered hand

the paradoxical point of beginning
        so that we might end, of loving
so that we might lose,
        the irrelevance that in this hand
declares that what is lost
        is not refound?

Reflexive, still, inconsequent the rage
        that tutors feeling to his corrected page,
measuring his skill not to confine
        but to unleash. Here, in
this room, a not dissimilar
        pen and dye make their

exclusion of what
        does not feel and does not
think, in feeling right and feeling good
        to find in opposites the move
of what he finds already there,
        quaint contraries to familiar despair.

He moves:
        below, the quaint conjectures
of his landlord's life:
        a call to servant, children, or his wife
— his own in Stratford
        where he sees his family's

re-endowment moved
        by celerity,
fortune, and the rest.
        He writes.
He shifts: reflexive, still, inconsequent the rage
        that tutors feeling to his conquered page.

The Age of Extinction

Changes furl inside this
ancient skull,
measure the pace,
re-constitute the shell
and shape, the furies
and delights, the irreparable
which is already there —
furl into the kingdom where
burnings shadow and reveal
the quivering and the stark.
The fashioned and unfashioned
edge what was there and
is, the catafalque prepared,
waiting to be used,
hollowed, bare, ungarlanded,
glistening in the dark.

Night-Head

Brittle
these charred cells
that rattle
in the head,
fear of fear
that tosses in:
fear furthering
into fear this
refurbishment
of terror.

Obituary

No:
these re-awakenings
will not arrest
what we learn late,
that dying's
best.
It doesn't matter what
you say or do:
no
inference is half so strong
as proving one another wrong
– wrong principle involved, or
what you feel or
what you think is felt more
deeply,
thought more closely,
fashioned to a greater
sense that what is real and what is true
is only to be seen by you.

Anniversary

The levity of flesh, faithful
to a sweet sensation
that buckles
heart to leave, in issue,
that further flesh:
this anniversal rucking,
his hand in hers,
hers on his cock,
his finger sheened so
she might say, 'So
that is all it was?'

To Find We Labour All the While

to measure out
our purpose to
our imaginings.

All else is lost:
the penalty we pay
provisioning despair

as, at a festival,
we hurry,
warily,
to greet our brothers.

Two of Everything

Two of everything
       he had:
two lips,
       two eyes,
two ears,
       a pair of arms,
a pair of legs,
       two thumbs,
ten toes
       (divisible by five)
(five fingers on each hand),
       two feet.

One nose:
       two nostrils.
One cock:
       two balls.
One arse:
       two cheeks.
One head:
       two minds.
One heart:
       four valves:
as if a bifurcated Prime Creator
       did everything by halves.

Revolution

Available to die:
my contemporaries
already are. I
have come to life through
them as they through
me. So literature
and art have spent such
forces in
their time
while I
am moving
to my prime:

fear turned to reason, guilt to sense,
     no longer shadowed by pretence
of who might like it, who might not
     (never at the best a lot):
minimum effect for maximum display
     never, as for others, came my way.
I laboured long but little came
     from what was best, no tame
competitor in stakes of fashion
     where little to be gained from passion.
Constraint in me no more prevails:
     the dead instruct, the dead retail
what I must know of their intent
     the better their wisdom to present:
'nutters' in vernacular speech
     where common aims inclined to meet
the better this wisdom to despite
     and turn such lightness into night.

They gave their best to what they may
        in being outcasts: not to say
they hadn't in their common dread
        the terrors of their midnight fed
by being here yet still apart
        from genial instinct to impart
that what is true must be in thrall
        to what is best and good for all.
Pissed on and shat on in their turn,
        they lined up only to confirm
that being brave is being strong
        in face of those they lived among:
truth lay, they found, as truth below
        the level that the public know.
Such fellow-marchers now are dead,
        revilers move up in their stead:
I march – and if I march alone
        know where they failed I am the one
survivor who, in final cast,
        will measure out their truth at last.
For what is this I see move in
        but others who see truth as sin
and where we ended they begin
        to unravel truth as if from lies
while us old truthsters they despise,
        damning us in later eyes
as if to say we found too late
        that, though we loved, we came to hate
to see our progress fade and die
        for want of yet another lie.

242

So mercenaries, we, of truth extolled,
        find change for change's sake unfold
all that our enemies foretold:
        we were not marching here to die
but merely to invent a lie
        to precede the lie that is to come
whenever revolution's won.
        We suffered long, we suffered hard
to find in struggle our reward
        is knowing less than we began
how man hands chaos on to man.
        What I decline to fight for now
is world made better by such row
        as fighters canvass day and night
the better instinct to requite:
        to come as instruments of good
and end as tools
        for other fools
to barter for our blood.

Necessity

The evil that men
do lives on,
re-charged
at each successive wave,
remorseless as the good, prayed
to destruction, to lead
our spectre on: the stone-eyed
god that sees such good betrayed
(phantasmal as the feast
that evil battens on in this
endless ghost parade):
the soundless beating at
the door, uncalled, unblessed,
as world without
such good is evil-less.

You and I

Evil thrives
as good survives:
without the one
there is no sum
to measure how
the good bestow
the bad upon
the simpleton;
for what we know
is evils grow,
and when we end
the good pretend
that what is good
is here to stay
— yet only beggars
kneel to pray.

This is true
for me and you,
that life is pain
and little gain:
for God's display
we have to pay
(as God's delight
is us to fright):
so God's remorse
is us to curse
as we return
from worm to worm,
until we breed
beyond our need,

and end our span
where we began,
in soil and ash
as heaven's trash:
no other show
but how we go,
(beyond recall
our final fall).

It isn't bad
that we've been had,
not even sad
that we are mad
(for God's arranged
that we're deranged)
— though still confused
that we've been used,
as in the end
we all must bend:
no grave allows
what grace avows,
since God's conceit
is our defeat
(his darkness sends
as he pretends
his darkness is
our only light).

The Final Visitor

What could he grasp?
The merciless provider
here at last

moved where no one
had removed before
the insidious intruder
with her eye of stone

the corporeal descendant
of incorporeal part
that tutored life to sanity
as death to heart

a once-loved visitant
who shadowed life to be
within each kiss and binding
the sting of misery

removed and then departed
the oncoming love to greet
each cherished love to harass or
to marry her defeat.

Purpose

The rabbit fears
what the stoat reveres.

A God made both
(for what it's worth).

Both pain and joy
in His employ.

What birth is this
to be His toy?

Stabat Pater

Did not Jesus say
at some point to the man
who was
      his mother's husband:
'What shall I do?'
and the man
      who was
her husband sighed,
'Pray that God is good to you'?

Did not Jesus in his life address,
at some point, the man
who was
      his mother's husband, thus:
'Father, I have sinned',
and the man
      who was
her husband sighed,
'Pray that God is good to you'?

Did not, at some point, Jesus
on the cross
      confess
to carpenter below
      who was
the man who was his mother's husband,
'Remember, now, the wood we used?'
and the man who was her husband sighed,
'Pray that God is good to you'?

Did not Jesus crucified
remember twice the man
who sighed
        and cry
to see him turn aside,
'Pray that God is good to you'?

Did not Jesus, taken dead,
resurrected,
        raise his head
and cry,
        at some point,
to the man
        who was
his mother's husband, 'Father: why?'
Pray that God is good to you.

The Mystery

Yes: many came in:
earlier than
we had thought,
more than we expected:
more than
we could count:
our beloved,
he amongst them:
all came in,
more than we could count,
so many entering as
they would the home that was
their home-place too, arriving
sooner than we thought:
the necessary calling,
the necessary sound,
the necessary hiding
of where the child was bound
as, years later, pinioned not
in a manger but
crossed on the timber
that a carpenter
had found.

Vespers

O come, dear God, and be our friend
and bring our torment to an end:

let us declare
that our despair
is only there
to bless the light.

I have nowhere to go:
this feeling comes: no
place to find:
here we decline

into the night,
into the night,

lest we portray
as we delay
what night intends
to sweep away.

Here we repine,
here we select
what prayers refine,
what prayers elect.

Ships move their course,
their anchorage change:
shallows converge.

These calls
that come in with the tide,
calls
from the shoal at the river
mouth: the slide
of sea across the sand:
a boat arrests the bay.

Each evening, Vesper comes.

No evening without such movement,
no nightly call
but the star's portrayal
in the pool or wave:
light pushed up cold against the warmth
of lamps along the promenade.

Vesper comes transposed
to this dull glow as
supplement to
moon and sun-last-light,
last flow to the movement
of the sea and swell.

Leave all behind,
leave all behind:

the star is right: the light is here;
here where the evening meadows into night,
lays fields of darkness to a darker hell.

Final Prayer

The sentence that we carry out
is what our genes are all about:
first in decline, and then in fast,
we live in tumult to the last:
so much essayed, so little 'chieved,
our lives, at death, so little grieved.

Those faces gazing out belie
what might be seen by calmer eye:
two faces gracious in their turn
from smiling-out to taciturn.

Instilled, becalmed, provoked, re-born,
between things learned and unlearned torn:
the smile of one, the wonder of the other,
as son turns into saviour, brother.

As beast in jungle summoning its prey,
depletes the goodness that it comes upon,
so God may marvel in his right
to make of earth eternal night:
for all that live as all that die
subscribe, in darkness, to his mystery.

Widow

Rests in the night as in
this dark: the woman
in her room across the backs
walks in a circle, her husband
dead, now she alone:
pores over sink, pores over depths
of her domestic pond,
eccentric in extreme, blind
to her window
which, with her unshaded bulb,
lights up across the yard
her scene: the round
of kitchen floor before
she contemplates a kettle,
then, in fit of terror,
shakes, as febrile as a dying
leaf: delicate as stamens
her bared arms, rodding
at her eyes.

She dies
each night a little in
his death, an involuntary decline
into where she calls and
mutters, wails alone
with her solitary
kettle on a solitary
stove: enveloping steam
haloes her sprung,
protruding hair, thrust up in
incandescence.

ii

Why should I speculate
on what, each night,
consumes her? This is not
for her alone,
what battens most on bone:
that frightening wake not
into delirium but
the brightness that invites
the brain to what is
fearful, unlooked-upon:
a mindless circling in an empty room,
a re-enclosure by
what she is invited to, a cry
that sucks the lung to leave a dread
greater than the fear
circling beneath
the eagle eye
that made that fear

and then abandoned it. What is
the privilege to see how
she despairs, takes
in the blow
that mendacity has struck ('Life is
worth living: I am
here to stay'), now
quarrelling with the one
who put her here: 'Why
me — when he was all I
had?' She bleeds invisibly
each night, a
phantasmagoria
of her most frequent fears.

God who has no care
protect her.

Re-visited

Here, on each successive
trip, we watch the sun subside
behind the moorland on
the opposite shore: a coruscation
of silhouetted slope and
slow ascending ground,
interjected amongst the green
and red, a fluorescence
that colours the estuary mouth,
disturbing the sea as it bares
its long enclosure
of reflected light. Clouds threaten
then outface the sun:
darkness curtains from the east
a pin-prick of first
light to witness, finitely, our
presence here —

here, where we lie,
matching eye to eye
what once was passion
but is now routine,
as predictable as a sleep
or our divergence from
a centred bed.

Modest pleasures mark us:
an enclosure of what was
unfathomed, unfettered, scarcely-
done, finding — in the clarity
that time fits on the least of these — our
indiscretions focused here
in sea and land and stranded vapour
that first reflects then shadows
light. A fissure opens where the darkness
starts, hollowed, sombre and intense:
the moon presents itself behind
black cloud — an
interlocutory light — until
the luminescent lip and
rounded edge flare whitely —
an incision in the sky which quickly
fades. Moments of that light
arrest each clouded edge:
beams moonrise on this flooding
tide creeping to the land in
eerie flow. We lie in
moonlight: two figures
consumed by that inclement
glow that coldly feels each mound
and dip, each severance
of the flesh, the stowing
of each shape inside the next,
one fitting-on, one fitting-in:
ghosts that measure
and re-tell what confiscature
of such feeling is, or was.

Moonrise is
a sultry thing, rising
in the darkness
to foretell what sun in
daylight has already lost
— a gamble
as to what it should resemble
in the absence of such light
to disassemble
my body out of yours (around
a right to move invisibly a form
— how firm, how strong — to where
each gazes on the other's
moonlit, catastrophic, sunless eye).
All things move invisibly
but these (the moonlit gantry
of our will — fabulous
in its isolation), as we address
a ghost that murmurs
with our voice and breath.
Here we reside in
florid light hung
weirdly in the window
of a ghostly room
— this pale, reflecting, opalescent
dust that counters our not
being here to being measureless,
inconsequent:
truthful to the truthless,
deadly to the deathless,
lively to the lifeless,
loving to the living.

We rest, set
out our camp,
lay out our bed,
conspire in our last
movement as our first
to fashion light from
love as moon
to dark lays out its luminescence
to declare that darkness
has an end.

The Tree

The tree is dark:
a tributary of the land.
For this is winter, love, and
bare, the last leaves gone
and something the far
side of despair
measures where,
throughout the summer,
we repaired
an animistic dread
(our mind
and body one).
This summoning
of what lies deepest:
a branch, a trunk, prefiguring
a deeper darkness.
We have loved the shell
of what our shuddering
and our feeling fill:
the sight of where
we gathered, lay,
canopied and capered,
lyrical and light. Here
no successor's song propels
that old conjecture
to distil the dark
— to proceed to the flame that
we subtend to make
our greater darkness
lighter yet.

Animals

Not sure where animals like this can go:
caged lemur, leopard, pacing
at the bar: the humanary flow
that waves, framing
its discretionary flight
to where the cageless captives nightly sight
the dreamsters' dreams of bestial delight
or plunge to a wickedness below
which bestiality itself must never go.

Remains, this creature
of the rail that plays
its internment in each
fractured space: forages
anew
and nightly gapes
at these, its terrible ferocities,
barred to the few,
feigning signals that govern
and declare that living
at extremities
as phantasmagorical as this
is beyond the reach of symmetry or bliss:

the most appalling consequence of all
when the last of these, our terrors, pall.

Where

Where does it come from,
where does it go,
this feeling of having
lived often before?

Why is it strong,
why does it last,
this feeling of having
more than one past?

Each time I awake,
each time I come round
from daydream or thinking
once more it is found.

Each life I have lived
has brought a distress
which memory fails
in each life to redress.

What each of these ghosts
of a life lived before
insists on reminding
is I have to live more.

Each death is the end
of a beginning begun
when death was the starting
of becoming a son.

Each time I re-track
this living I've had
— like mirror in mirrors
reflecting me back —

each time I awake,
each time that I die,
I look at the chaos
to be measured as I.

Each end a beginning
as beginning bequeaths
a perpetual longing
to die as I please.

Each end is the start
of beginning again
a lifetime of anguish
to be ended in pain.

Way of Sin

We have the time, we have the care
to meet then challenge our despair.

How the figuration of each moment
quells, then quivers — provisioning each step,
each quaint construction we erect or change
one moment to the next — to fare as now
no better than we might to glide across
a sea with our two loves to light where no
one shows the way — or free ourselves from what
each body ill-repairs in fissure and
erosure. This our despatch to where we
each must now begin to fathom good by
way of sin.

A Final Good

Each day re-measures where
I must begin: to censure
or depict where what is
reasoned takes its leave and fires
in each declining and repairing
light the contour of what, in loving,
lessens well
my
primogeniture amongst
the denizens of hell.

(Ask no better, nor
expect, for
darkness deepens light as well.)

Turn where such
madness weathers well
the dull declivities of hell:
the ditch and dyke that reason lays
and contours, less to delay
than to command
the source of each
nocturnal reprimand.
(For what is featured well
is damned.)
This purpose to our
madness pays its due
in saying what is hell
is good for you.

The Savage

I write from the death-house:
this is what I did;
what I do now no different,
nor is wrong — the body turning
in its bid to grasp
that dying, like our living,
is our last.

This strange emergence
burning for this while
to turn at this ferocity,
marked and marking
here to grasp
that this, our living,
is our last.

Uniquely marked, uniquely saved
until this savage in our path
yields to what nature
in this savagery foretells
that we are in the worst
of nature's hells.

Such residue that savagery declines
lives on in rescued minds
as nature to survivor casts this
the last of all its spells
to choose, in wisdom, to instil
this is the worst of all our hells.

God measures our despair
to seize what height descended
from must mean: as depth to such
must surely be as darkness
to a light its brilliance.

So shines our dark
and guides our spell
of living out our hope in hell,
our faith in what our living seems
that dark is all that darkness means
to mark our blackness for ourselves.

This torture to the torturer tell
to be a partner in our hell,
to here descend,
our pain commend
to find such darkness in himself.

This is the savage that we find as
purpose to our purposelessness;
there is no greater love than this
to find in pain and then confess
that love is loved by lovelessness.

Tree

The tree shakes: it shudders,
braced, invisibly, below us
from this high window where,
in bed, we lie,
constrained by what the winter,
leafless, tells:
this is the least of all our hells.

Leaf-ful, we have watched it rise,
burdened lightly by what it greenly flies,
fluttered to the morning spells
of breeze and sunlight
here in the least of all our hells.

Here we have looked at,
through and inbetween
— dawn, dusk — and seen
the levity with which it
guides not only what it
will be but has been,
here in the least of all our hells.

Now, bereft, it staunchly flies
at, against, into the winter skies:
shows, starkly, where its armature
has seen, felt rupture,
tear, yet prospers well
here, in the least of all our hells.

We lie, honed to our love as
to a bed that faces,
in the frame of our two selves,
such likened life that winters
here till Spring foretells
once more the least of all our hells.

We drive and torture,
unwittingly commune
with what the summers
breed and autumns fell
here amongst the least of all our hells.

If heaven rises with the light that
flies on naked branch and trunk and shell
of what the tree so treely brought
each day, each spring and summer to
ourselves, then does it too
here amongst the least of all our hells.

Stark monument or rivulet
of sky, fissured
to a greater brightness yet
than that defined
by darkness darker than
this the least of all our hells.

We purpose that we shed
our leaf as well,
reduce our nature to a frieze
as when at darkest moment
of the year we tell

this is not in any way our hell
but, in constancy of loving well,
light in our darkness here amongst
what was once
the least of all our hells.

She: Older than the Century, 1991

Yes, she is there: older
than the century,
as if each year
draws closer
to where her
love is found, here
where I have known her:
more sudden
in repose, here
where the loving
flows, where the flesh
invades, reminding
where the present grows, re-shaping
thought and touch
to where the lip is
still, the cheek is
still, the hand quavers
still, the features
favoured more by time than
age can
hold: she is loved, the source
and centre,
deeper, wider
in her grasp
that we have heaven
here at last.

She rises with the sun,
a darkness in our darkness
to outrun;
this, where time might
otherwise have lost
all that fleshliness
itself has cost
− unflinching in her raptured smile
as, rapturous,
she our raptures whiles
to a sense of endlessness.

INDEX